THE WAY WE SEE IT

THE WAY WE SEE IT

Sandra Richards

Trentham Books
Stoke on Trent, UK and Sterling, USA

Trentham Books Limited
Westview House   22883 Quicksilver Drive
734 London Road   Sterling
Oakhill   VA 20166-2012
Stoke on Trent   USA
Staffordshire
England ST4 5NP

© 2008 Sandra Richards

First published 2008

British Library Cataloguing-in-Publication Data
A catalogue record for this book is available from the British Library

ISBN: 978 1 85856 420 3

Cover photograph: Djanomi Fulani (aged 10, Year 5)
by Sandra Richards

Designed and typeset by Trentham Print Design Ltd, Chester and printed in Great Britain by Hobbs the Printers Ltd, Hampshire.

From Diane Abbott MP

This is an interesting book that raises some important points about the British education system and its relationship with Afro-Caribbean children and their communities. The book rightly focuses on the importance of the formation of identity in young people's lives. The dearth of positive role models, negative media images and the effects of living in a post-colonialist era are all drawn upon to illustrate how young black people's identities are in crisis. The analysis Dr. Richards makes of the trauma that parents suffer as a result of their own and their children's experiences in school is also notable, and I particularly agree with her recommendation that teachers must develop emotional literacy in order to give the best opportunities to all pupils.

*This book is dedicated to the memory of my daughter
June Estine and my Godson Simon George Patterson*

*I also want to dedicate it to the millions of students past, present and future
who are denied equal access to an education that nurtures their full holistic
potential through no fault of their own. Particularly the memory of those like
Jevan Richardson who committed suicide to escape. It forms part of the legacy
bestowed in recognition of the tireless efforts of countless practitioners, parents,
politicians and other activists who have worked and continue to work tirelessly
toward inclusive paradigms, inclusive practice and raising the achievement of
all, regardless of socially constructed classifications.*

*The book is dedicated also to the non-biological children I am constantly being
blessed with, like the thousands of children penalised for exhibiting behavioural
symptoms – an obvious response to psychological trauma caused by devastating
events of life, such as war, divorce, death, illness, puberty, discrimination and
exclusion. And to our homegrown mentors like my community son Auron
Tannice (African Ambassador and guide) and my community son Kinyatta, a
fine young man from Uganda who was awarded a scholarship to a boarding
school in East Sussex, where they called him George because from their
perspective his name should be George Kinyatta and not Kinyatta George.*

Contents

The author's voice

All we can see is just social injustice, violence and crime. (15 year-old British born Caribbean-African)

On 10 December 2006 *The Independent on Sunday* reported that:

Black pupils are three times more likely to be excluded than white and five times less likely to be on the official register of gifted and talented students. Why? Because, according to a Whitehall report, teachers in England and Wales are unconsciously prejudiced against Caribbean-origin pupils. http://education.independent.co.uk/news/article2062500. ece

On 9 July 2007 *New Nation* newspaper published an article in which African Oxford University graduate and broadcaster Henry Bonsu reminisced:

There were very few black faces when I was at Oxford University. Of course there were some African and American students, but the numbers of black British was pitiful and it probably hasn't changed much at Oxford or Cambridge.

Early in 2007 three youths were shot dead in south London within days of each other and although condolences are extended to the bereaved families of the thousands of people affected by increasing youth conflict, including the family and friends of 15 year-old Michael Dosunmu who was shot in his own bed, nothing can bring them back or explain the pain of losing a child physically, emotionally, spiritually or psychologically. Sadly, since writing this preface more young people have lost their lives and the opportunities education brings. Those that are left are increasingly exposed to drugs and guns. During an event called Black Question Time on 27 October 2007, Superintendent Leroy Logan reported that some 75 per cent of DNA held on the police database is from black minority ethnic communities.

> *Every time I hear of another murder, I say to myself: please God don't let it be another young black person.* (Diasporan grandfather)

Young people are exposed to conflict they seem unable to resolve peacefully; they are losing hope and their families are full of grief and despair. There is clearly a missing link between young people in school and young people in a world outside of school.

Youth workers, mentors and other practitioners who work closely with young people, have a perspective seldom revealed that can provide an insight into the world and perspectives of many young people.

> *I saw him a couple of days after the incident and asked him if he didn't see me there. He said he didn't. When they are upset they just see red. That's why I think it's important to work with them and give them strategies to stay out of dangerous situations. People think it's just black kids stabbing and shooting, it's not, they're all angry, bored and demanding respect.* (Youth worker)

Although the Caribbean African community is clearly the worst affected, the consequences of this trend of youth violence and school exclusion is disastrous for everybody as this escalating phenomenon is certain to spill into wider society and we can ill afford to abandon young people. They are our children, our sons, daughters, brothers, sisters, nephews, nieces, grandchildren or the friends and peers of our offspring.

Research indicates that there is a link between school exclusion, disaffection and vulnerability to crime, unemployment and reduced opportunities. There has been much research in this area showing that too many students, in particular Caribbean African boys, are excluded but there has been less work that has braved the professional risk and personal discomfort of presenting the voice of the practitioner, the excluded young people and the parent who was excluded as a child and continues to be excluded as a parent.

Whilst there is some good work in schools, clearly something is fundamentally wrong. This is a state of emergency yet no-one seems to care enough to do something to unearth the cause. They are more concerned with sticky plastering over the symptom. Parents are observing that the government is too complacent and not working to empower parents.

Too much research, too little action. Social services inna wi business an naah listen. We are taking the blame and the government are too laid back but what sweet nanny goat ah goh run im belly. (Great Grandparent)

Whilst it can be argued that many children are achieving and that, in the words of member of parliament, David Lammy:

It's not helpful to stereotype all black boys as failing – many are succeeding. (David Lammy, MP for Tottenham)

Too high a percentage of young people are being failed by the education system.

Sticking a plaster over a gaping wound that has led to what the Conservative party leader describes as a broken society will not bring about the needed community cohesion and social inclusion Labour says they are working toward.

I have found that good citizens and great teachers have been hoodwinked by the paradigms and practices that are not enough to put things right, so it is time for a re-examination of an old issue. This prompted my research.

This book is the product of qualitative research designed to avoid blaming but instead identify solutions and provide a platform to the community most adversely affected by a teaching phenomenon of excluding children who have a right to an excellent education. *The Way We See It* calls for a fresh look at school exclusion and dares to present the uncomfortable but much-needed discourse that unpicks certain issues in an attempt to identify root causes of exclusion and begin identifying solutions that will give all children the right to equal education, decent housing, employment opportunities, abundance and good health. The phrase most used in this book is 'social inclusion'. It may be used interchangeably with integration. Integration is about a pupil's readiness for being placed in (or returned to) mainstream education.

The comments of young Caribbean Africans provide valuable insight into the world of some of the most educationally marginalised and vulnerable young people, along with their parents, the community they come from and the practitioners who work with pupils who are excluded or at risk of exclusion. It is the way they see it.

Although I recognise black as a political term which related to Asians and Africans and means non-white, I use the word African to refer to persons of African heritage because I recognise that people can be British, born into a Caribbean culture and be of African heritage. I also believe that to be African-centred includes the need not only to re-frame existing paradigms but also to re-orientate and re-form language. Africans are not a homogenous group, so definitions are problematic. Black British, African Caribbean, Caribbean, Black African, African Other, Mixed Heritage, Dual Heritage are all inadequate terms, as difficulties exist with broad based definitions which could apply to many young people because the meaning of the term is not agreed. Many communities are rejecting such labels and blanket terms like 'urban', because these are externally imposed terms that do not value people's heritage or identity.

A person's ability to develop a sense of self that is appropriate to their cultural origin is determined by how much they are told about their history. The use of the terms black or non-white, which set people in oppositional contrast to white is negative and, more importantly it dehumanises and bears no relation to place of origin (Welsing, 1995). A more useful description relates people to their history and to their geographical place of origin. No people can be spiritually and culturally secure without some notion of historical origin and tradition.

Using the word African to describe those of us generally referred to as black includes but is not limited to Africans born on the continent of Africa, in the Caribbean, in Europe or anywhere else in the Diaspora and includes Africans with dual or mixed heritage and anyone typically labelled with the colour coded description black. However I use the word black when necessary to make a point, as I recognise that black is also a pan-African statement of liberated consciousness. British born Afrikan scholar William Lezlee Lyrics Henry argues BLAK (black liberation African knowledge) is a concept which empowers a largely disempowered community.

> .....blak, is a self-generated concept [that] represents the real need to embrace a more positive notion of an Afrikan/blak self as a tool for negotiating a sane path through a hostile, racist, environment. (Henry, 2006)

In response to research findings, I also rename some familiar terms, for example the words slave and slavery are replaced where appropriate with the words enslaved and enslavement, to shift the emphasis onto a dehumanising crime against humanity rather than a respectable business transaction in human trafficking.

This book seeks to reveal fundamental social inequalities and generational prejudice cloaked in the respectability of pleasantries, false smiles and highly regarded qualifications. It is time to deal with a traumatic incident that took place in British and African history, the legacy of which still lurks, causing a situation where students, teachers, families and society are prickly about education injustices. If we remain unclear about the cause and nature of an injury we cannot introduce appropriate interventions.

The Way We See It opens up a sensitive veiled system of education, by showing it from the viewpoint of students, practitioners, parents whose opinion is usually contested although disguised by an illusion of inclusion when the conversation could be too difficult for teachers.

> The inner eye provides not only a racialised vision of the world, it also creates a particular orientation in the teacher in social class terms. This has its roots in the class divisions of the society and also in the specific history of education in Britain. Although student teachers are generally familiarised with this history, seldom are they asked to reflect on their identities as (white) middle class professionals and ask themselves how this might affect their dealing with (black) working class students. (Maud Blair, 2001)

1

Exclusion, inclusion and discrimination in schools

My child suffered so much that I prayed the Lord would take us both. I feel so much guilt now that I just let her shout at me if she wants to. (Parent of an excluded child)

Introduction

Rates of exclusion remain significantly higher for black students than for any other group except Travellers. In November 2005 the Department for Education and Skills (DfES) identified exclusions of black children as a priority area for action. Late in 2006 an internal review document called Getting it. Getting It Right focusing on the exclusion of African pupils was made public.

Getting it. Getting It Right recognised the possibility that official exclusion data masks a wider unofficial exclusions gap and that decreases in official exclusion statistics could be masking increases in unofficial exclusions. It also noted that African pupils are disciplined more frequently and more harshly. A key decision in the report was around the impact of racism which was referred to as the R-word and the possible consequences for organisations that 'got it' or 'didn't get it'. This is still tiptoeing and walking on eggshells around a glaring fact that school exclusion is strongly linked to race and gender evidenced by the disturbing absence of the mere word racism.

This evidence challenges the assumption that racial inequalities in education are merely a reflection of socioeconomic inequalities in society. It

1

makes a compelling case for the existence of an 'X-factor', related to ethnicity, which explains the exclusions gap. (DfES, 2006)

Getting it. Getting It Right presents conservative figures indicating that that black Caribbean pupils are three times more likely to be excluded from school than white pupils. When free school meals and special education needs are taken into account Caribbean African pupils are still more than two and a half times more likely to be excluded from school than their peers. In addition African pupils are more likely to be considered as having special education needs, free school meals, longer and more numerous previous exclusions, poor attendance records, criminal records and being looked after by social services (Parsons *et al*, 2000, Ofsted). The document says little about the consequences for wider society, once again placing cause and consequence in the African community. Here is yet another review that does not take a bold enough look at the possible underlying causes and solutions. Instead, condescendingly, it refers to a mysterious X-factor.

The prison service offers a lifelong career choice to many excluded young people. Some become career inmates controlled by those who have chosen the prison service as an employment career option. Many young people view the prison service as a lucrative source of revenue for many and a way that the government continues exercising control and maintaining exclusion.

> *Look ... Europe prefers animals to children ... eats its young, sends them up chimneys, leaves them unattended so why should they care about us. A lot of business is made off strife. Money is being made on the street that feed off kids killing kids. Justice system, police and stuff. They don't care they're making money off it.* (Excluded young man)

In the words of Martin Narey, Director General of HM Prison Service (2001):

> *The 13,000 young people excluded from school each year might as well be given a date by which to join the prison service some time later down the line.*

Without education it is difficult to find employment and social movement is restricted. Trapping people in an environment without skills, knowledge or money arrests their development. Arrested development and economic hardship can lead to poverty, rendering people unable to travel or broaden their horizons. More relevant to marginalised people, restricted movement prevents the renewing and healing of severed relationships with siblings, grandparents and other family members from their cultural community. In addition many families experience high levels of anxiety caused by their children's schooling.

There is growing acknowledgement of the value of multi-agency collaborations but how this works in practice eludes many organisations. Moreover, there is increasing evidence to show that existing helping models are often ineffective and may even be oppressive. Consequently, there is a real need for alternative worldviews to be used as the basis of helping develop paradigms with practices that value collectivism and adopt two or more approaches instead of only one way of seeing things. The model that emerges from my research provides a more ecological approach to practice. Ruddick (2000) argues that to make a major difference in a young person's life schools must become more ecological and acknowledge that there are factors outside the child which have an impact on achievement.

A negative experience of school can have lasting effects. It can lead to low self-esteem and low expectations and, in turn, to: anti-social behaviour orders, unemployment, impoverishment, ill-health and mental disorder, more teenage pregnancies; drugs and crime in youth culture. Hopelessness and despair might well be traced back to childhood experiences.

This book presents insights into the way young people operate in their worlds and what they say in their private safe spaces. It explains why the description 'black' or 'ethnic minority' has no meaning for increasing members of the Caribbean African community. It makes the link between exclusion, colonialism and the period of African enslavement.

The future prospects of young people who have been excluded or who underachieve in British schools are bleak. There is evidence to suggest that children who have been excluded from school are more likely to be unemployed and are at greater risk of serving time incarcerated at her majesty's pleasure. The young people who are not imprisoned dodge bullets and the hurtful remarks of adults who blame young people entirely for the plight of being young in today's world.

My friend got jumped for his phone. I don't go into areas where I don't know anyone, I stay in my ends. Adults blame us for everything and blank us. We didn't start it, it's just how it goes. (British born African male)

Dr Joy DeGruy Leary (2005) lists the symptoms she found in people suffering from post-traumatic stress disorder:

- concern about serious threat or harm to one's life or physical integrity

- fearing harm to one's children, spouse or close relative

- stress experienced with intense fear, terror and helplessness

- physiological reactivity on exposure to internal or external cues

- markedly diminished interest or participation in significant activities.

- feeling of detachment or estrangement from others

- sense of foreshortened future (does not expect to have a career, marriage, children or normal lifespan)

- irritability or outbursts of anger

- difficulty concentrating

Having been repeatedly confronted with shocking school exclusion statistics, I decided to investigate. I discovered alarmingly similar trauma indicators to those identified by DeGruy Leary. I found that:

- school exclusion and psychological bullying affects certain communities disproportionately, reducing their opportunity to gain qualifications and secure employment, access housing, avoid poverty and ill health

- increasing numbers of students and parents know that African boys are more likely than others to be excluded

- parents are anxious about their children's self-esteem at school

- parents and pupils feel disempowered and parents feel helpless to support their children to achieve their full potential

- nervousness and clumsy dialogue between parents and teachers create misunderstandings and accusations by teachers that African parents are aggressive

4

- disengagement of parents from school activities is interpreted by schools as lack of interest

- parents are perceived as a hostile enemy creating difficulties in developing healthy equal partnerships between parents and teachers

- teachers refuse to recognise their mistakes and make amends

- young people and parents are less able to endure what they perceive as education social injustice or disrespect because of enduring tensions

- the impact on generations of marginalised people outside the classroom affects the preparedness and ability of students to relax and learn. Consequently, they may have difficulty in concentrating on lessons

On further investigation, I identified the people most adversely affected in schools and the factors affecting today's exclusion figures. I have revealed the human stories that emerged, and have proposed practical solutions from the point of view of those most vulnerable to school exclusion, their parents and the practitioners who work to keep them included.

I uncovered new information about a history that has led to what Diane Abbott MP describes as the 'silent catastrophe' affecting Caribbean African students (*Observer*, 6.1.2002). I discovered how thousands of Caribbean African children are pathologised by a legacy they have inherited, as revealed in 1971 by Bernard Coard in his seminal book *How the West Indian child is made educationally sub-normal in the British school system*. I also made some intriguing discoveries about how young people adapt modern day language and culture and use technology to survive and communicate in their own worlds.

In addition to making alarming links with Dr DeGruy Leary's work (2005), I was struck by the link to post-colonial trauma and enduring stress. I also became aware of a deep sadness and regret in the diasporan community similar to grieving.

I had to wait till I left school to get any qualifications. The only other black person I saw was in the canteen. I didn't know anything about my history and I am angry with my parents and myself. My mum never did biology,

5

chemistry or history neither did my Dad so I can't really blame them. They are sorry and sad, so am I. (African university lecturer)

What is happening in schools affects a community of adults who are parents of children at risk of exclusion and who may themselves have been excluded as children. The implications for the community and for society are grave, and my research seeks to shed light on how this discrimination can be brought to an end.

An African-centred research paradigm

Centrism is the operation of the person as subject (eg African as subject, Latino as subject, European as subject) and has two components: theory and practice. It is possible to master one and not the other, to be involved in the theory and not in the practice or vice versa. One can have a historical and social memory that is not culturally African but practice Afrocentricity as a life style and pursue a world voice, which is Africa-centred in relation to external phenomena. Not distinctly African, but Africa-centred, a theoretical perspective. This approach to theoretical perspectives avoids notions of one as better than the other. Instead, centrism recognises and acknowledges alternative knowledge and places the holder of the particular perspective as central to the worldview.

Unconscious revelations surfaced during dynamic conversations with my university supervisor and researcher colleagues who were interrogating this work. The methodological approach facilitated a constant comparison between data and research direction. It also facilitated my analysis of field notes and journal entry cross-overs. This approach unveiled reflections I had found difficult to access when writing in solitude. This technique was chosen as a conscious African-centred technique in the tradition of Africans as oral folk and was a process used to capture deeper unconscious revelations than simply keeping a journal could.

Exclusion is not simply a matter of physical or technical marginalisation. Indeed, as race has been found to be a significant factor in UK school exclusion, to exclude an African philosophical worldview would have hampered the research. I avoided perpetrating the usual practice of researching and analysing African situations using European philosophical worldviews. African-centered perspective emerges from African life. Its existence is found in the inter-generational transmissions of African peoples.

I use the lens of academia (Henry, 2006) through which to present an insider perspective and analyse narratives. I am screened and questioned by the people I interview so that I will not misrepresent or betray them and our Ancestors. I adopt a centrist position.

My research took an African-centred philosophical approach throughout, using appropriate interrelated methods that allowed me to capture unconscious revelations. Placed at the centre, I could reveal a new perspective on the longstanding problem of exclusion.

Exclusion

Exclusion is another word for rejection. It can affect people of differing skin colour, age, religion, gender, social class, orientation, worldview, ability and culture. Variables such as gender, class and ethnicity increase the risk of exclusion for some pupils. Sadly these variables are often known to researchers, policy makers and teachers but are unknown to parents, guardians and children.

DfES guidelines advise that a decision to exclude a pupil should be taken only:

- in response to serious breaches of the school's behaviour policy

- if allowing the pupil to remain in school would seriously harm the education or welfare of the pupil or others in the school. http://www.teachernet.gov.uk/wholeschool/behaviour/exclus ion/guidance/part2

There are a number of ways to exclude and be excluded. When the topic of exclusion is raised it often conjures up the notion of formal exclusion which is an official term for the removal of a child from access to education buildings but not the education curriculum *per se*. An excluded student should still receive full access to the national curriculum even if not physically permitted inside a school building or on school premises.

State schools are governed by central government legislation and local government (LEA) recommendations. State schools operate two different types of exclusion, fixed term and permanent.

Fixed exclusion can be of any length and for up to 45 school days in any one academic year so long as the aggregate of fixed period exclusions for the pupil does not exceed the total of 45 in any one academic year according to strict guidelines laid down by the Department for Education and Skills (DfES). Formal exclusion is only one form of exclusion: it can be permanent, or a fixed term exclusion, which is a suspension from accessing school buildings for a determined length of time.

Other forms of exclusion are manifest in:

- the practices of professionals who withhold the curriculum, penalising children by placing them outside classrooms or in offices as a punishment

- policies that separate children on the basis of success and failure

- disengagement of students themselves from academic participation

- Discrimination due to skin colour, gender, class, religion, culture, ability, sexual orientation, age, personality clash or other excessive abuses of power such as excessive and disproportionate application of school rules.

It can be hard to identify when exclusion is an act of discrimination – and hard to prove. But the impact of unequal access is real. For instance, a child may be on a school register and therefore a member of the school community attending classes but still experience education exclusion at the hands of professionals who skilfully abuse practices that appear to be in the interests of the child. Children can be appointed as monitors who run errands at crucial times of the school day or as peer mentors who may be gifted and talented but spend their time helping others instead of being helped to excel further themselves. You can tell whether or not these actions are exclusionary when the impact of these appointments is found to have no benefit to the child. The guidelines for exclusion are in DfES Circular 10/99 which introduces the processes and types of exclusion and the appeal procedures.

There is no established process for diagnosing the teacher-student relationship as possibly contributing to exclusion. Nor is there a systematic way of identifying children's learning needs that need to be met to take the pupil off the path to exclusion. The past record of teachers in excluding are ignored and the life experience of young people who may have already experienced racism, poverty, civil war or bereavement may be disregarded, leaving them to be further traumatised when teachers exclude them from school. Young people are blamed for unresolved problems, misunderstandings, personality conflicts or errors and become marginalised or excluded. Parents spoke of being 'badgered' by school secretaries and not being given sufficient time or information to appeal. In effect the child and family are subject to the will and power of the school whether or not the pupil is to blame.

> *It was just before the half-term break and the school rang my work to tell me my child was not to come back until the school decided.* (Parent)

Such information is often conveyed on a Friday, leaving the parent powerless for the weekend or even a longer period if the exclusion is made at the end of a term.

There appear to be huge areas of misunderstanding between students, teachers and parents which can escalate into tensions, mistrust and feed stereotypes. My research found many cases where children have been excluded because of avoidable misunderstandings.

The effects of disaffection both nationally and locally are all too evident. The DfES has the main responsibility for policy on truancy and exclusion, the Home Office has responsibility for crime and criminal justice and social services and the Department of Health have key interests in combating the impact of all of these. As the cost of social inclusion continues to rise, government is increasingly concerned to document the consequences or outcomes of educational interventions in the services they fund.

Considerable research focuses on school exclusions and social exclusion. Levitas (1998) offers three forms of discourse with reference to exclusion

- Redistributionist – the focusing on high profile social problems like begging.

- Moral Underclass – people's tendency to become dependent on benefits

■ Social Integration – identifying a correlation between people's lack of attachment to family, work, education and the degree of their exclusion. This can be described as disaffection

Exclusion can be voluntary or non-voluntary, that is self-imposed (internal) or imposed (external). The voluntary imposition of exclusion is due to individuals or groups opting out of the mainstream education system mentally, physically or emotionally. Opting out mentally might be through not attempting to engage in the academic and pastoral expectations of the education establishment. Opting out physically might be through truancy, psychosomatic illness or lateness whilst opting out emotionally might be related to anger, resentment, avoiding engagement, behavioural issues or through lack of confidence:

> When young people develop an overall positive self-concept, they become free and confident enough to go where their skills, desires and opportunities will take them. Success improves self-esteem and, eventually, the self-concept, thus making it easier to take on the next challenge or tolerate the occasional failure. (Comer, 1992)

> These voluntary and unofficial exclusions may far outnumber those that are officially recorded and reported. (Bourne *et al*, 1994)

Non-voluntary exclusion occurs by external mechanism. This may be through technical exclusion, which could take the form of disallowing the mainstream curriculum, withdrawing a student from classroom situations, keeping them on the education establishment register but placing them in off-site provision or visible physical exclusion from the premises of the school. When young people are described as disruptive, behaviourally or emotionally challenged they can become the victim of negative stereotyping because of their perceived identity. That their own personal and socio-cultural perspectives are ignored or marginalised is the first step to being excluded.

DfEE (1999) guidance on exclusions state that

> exclusion should be used only in response to serious breaches of a school's policy, when all other reasonable steps have been taken and is not appropriate for minor misconduct (such as occasional failure to do homework or bring dinner money) ... pregnancy is not in itself sufficient reason for exclusion.

Children who are permanently excluded should be quickly re-integrated into school wherever possible, but despite this DfEE recommendation statistics indicate that this happens in approximately one third of cases. Two thirds lose their entitlement to full-time education and receive what is known in education law as education otherwise usually in special centres.

The Government's education otherwise plans include the following targets:

> All children should have a clear individual education plan which includes a date for reintegration, further education or training as a more realistic aim for young people coming to the end of compulsory school.

Case studies

All my research shows, the gap between rhetoric and reality is vast, and children constantly fall between the two. There follow just three of the many cases revealed by my research. These examples may appear extreme but, sadly, they are not uncommon.

Terence is of mixed cultural heritage (Caribbean African and European English). At nursery he was shouted at by the class teacher, who did not realise that Terence has a hearing impairment. The teacher failed to identify the reason why Terence did not respond and interpreted it as defiance, punishing Terence and finally excluding him for a fixed term.

At 15 Taneisha was denied the opportunity to sit her exam because she wore the wrong tights to school. The school did not enquire as to the reason and so did not learn that there had been a house fire and Taneisha had lost most of her possessions. Her parents wanted her to have as normal a day as possible and not jeopardise her life chances by missing her exam, so they sent her to school even though she was not adhering to the school dress code.

Mrs. Jenkins was divorced and struggling to keep a home together for her three children. The eldest, a 13-year-old girl Simone, was not coping with her father's absence and began arriving at school late. The school called a meeting and Mrs. Jenkins arrived to find herself facing a special needs coordinator (SENCO), head of year, mentor, professional from the PRU and form tutor. The head of year read out a catalogue of Simone's alleged misdemeanours. The tone of the meeting caused Mrs. Jenkins to break down into tears.

Social Inclusion

Attendance at school is considered a prerequisite for pupils' progress, reducing disaffection, disenchantment and above all pupil's sense of failure and the impact on the individual and society at large.

In a report responding to the Brixton uprising in 1981, Lord Scarman pointed to the poverty, urban deprivation, racial discrimination and racial disadvantage he found in the community. He hoped to inform social policy, and warned that if these issues were not tackled, they would remain a potential trigger for further unrest (Scarman, 1981).

If we look at inclusion in its broader sense we can see many obstacles to its implementation. This is also the case in schools. In theory, primary and secondary schools support the need for inclusion. In practice, structural constraints, non-statutory requirements to include result in schools using exclusion as a penalty. This is a poor reflection on the teaching profession because in these situations exclusion is a way for teachers to opt out of their responsibility to treat all students equally.

> Inclusion is a recycling of old ideas with a shift in terminology the re-phrasing of inclusion is linguistic not conceptual: the discourse of inclusion is in itself exclusionary. (Mittler, 2000)

The concept of social inclusion was popularised in France in 1974 by Reni Lenoir, then secretary of state for social action, who recognised the need to strengthen social cohesion and improve conditions for those whom the economy was leaving behind. The term social inclusion was used in France to refer to people who were physically impaired, mentally challenged or socially maladjusted and applied to a similar population in the UK.

The 1981 Education Act, informed by the recommendations of the Warnock Report (1988), heralded a move away from applying a medical model approach to the child towards the context of learning. The DfES Code of Practice (2001) supports this focus. It advocates a policy of inclusive educating and recommends that the majority of children with special education needs difficulties should be educated within main-stream provision.

In schools a skilled Special Educational Needs Coordinator (SENCO), may prevent problems escalating and produce changes for the better. However, if the difficulty cannot be managed the school can and often does exclude the child. DfES guidelines recommend effective early intervention to prevent emerging problems from becoming special educational needs. There are three levels of recommended action: school action; school action plus external support (eg LA, health) and statement of learning needs (for the most severe learning difficulties).

Some needs – such as dyslexia or problems of attention and hyper-activity – require placement on the SEN register for assistance rather than exclusion which is a punishment. But much of the social inclusion procedure seems to be about isolating the disaffected.

Although social inclusion is driven by government, there seems to be no national body regulating social inclusion interventions. Interventions are not officially supported or centrally coordinated in terms of pro-vision, codes of practice or competence requirements. There are no published statistics of the number of social inclusion initiatives being funded or operating effectively and no one model or approach is advo-cated or recommended.

The inclusive education discourse in England is largely linked to chil-dren with special education needs (SEN). My research is not specifically concerned with SEN, but studied the pupils who are labelled SEN to satisfy budgetary requirements and the organisational needs of prac-titioners. Thus they are part of the marginalised community which this research is reviewing – something also noted by Coard in 1971. Then, as now, Caribbean African children were considered under-achievers and now instead of segregating them they are simply excluded, which has the same effect of devaluing and damaging people and their communi-ties. In the recent publication, *Tell It Like It Is* (Richardson, 2005) which reproduced Coard's work, distinguished researchers argued that, dis-turbingly, little has changed.

The government's Social Exclusion Unit (1998b) defines inclusion thus:

> Inclusive education practice consists of an approach which works creati-vely and effectively to counteract the challenges experienced by mar-ginalised groups. Inclusive education principles presuppose that main-stream school, where possible (or at least a mainstream education) is the best education placement/provision for young people. Young people who find mainstream school challenging are considered at risk or vul-nerable. If young people experience a combination of challenges, eg

social emotional, behavioural and attendance needs that are not met; this presents challenges to teachers, peers and their parents/carers that can escalate out of control. As a consequence young people may become excluded.

As the indicators for exclusion are measured in terms of economics, employment, delinquency, truancy, illegitimacy and teenage pregnancy, it is reasonable to assume that inclusion would be measured against the same indicators. The Social Exclusion Unit report (1998) suggests that getting young people into mainstream schools and the workforce constitutes social inclusion. However, there is a need for agreement about what good social inclusion practice should entail.

CSIE has developed an *Index for Inclusion* (CSIE, 2000) as a tool for schools to use. It is organised in three dimensions: culture, policy and practice:

- creating inclusive cultures (building community and establishing inclusive values)

- producing inclusive policies (developing school and organising support for diversity)

- evolving inclusive practice (orchestrating learning and mobilising resources)

The *Index for Inclusion* suggests that inclusion in education involves:

- valuing all students and staff equally

- increasing the participation of students in and reducing their exclusion from, the cultures, curricula and communities of local schools

- restructuring the cultures, policies and practices in schools so that they respond to the diversity of students in the locality

- reducing barriers to learning and participation for all students, not only those with impairments or those who are categorised as having special educational needs

- learning from attempts to overcome barriers to the access and participation of particular students to make changes for the benefit of students more widely

- viewing the difference between students as resources to support learning, rather than as problems to be overcome

- acknowledging the right of students to an education in their locality

- improving schools for staff as well as for students

- emphasising the role of schools in building community and developing values, as well as in increasing achievement

- fostering mutually sustaining relationships between schools and communities

- recognising that inclusion in education is one aspect of inclusion in society

- young people more likely to find mainstream school challenging are considered at risk

This index provides a framework for evaluation. However, social exclusion issues remain extremely complex, highly problematic and relatively controversial.

Certain factors are critical to re-integrating young people back into schools (Daniels *et al*, 2003). They have to have:

- belief in their own abilities

- supportive family and friends

- ongoing support from link workers or other skilled staff after permanent exclusion

Daniels (2003) asserts that re-integration into mainstream in schools often failed but that it was possible to achieve highly inclusive schools which had inclusion policies, practice and practitioners.

Mittler's (2000) finding that link-workers from a range of professional backgrounds can make a significant contribution to positive outcomes for young people is highly significant. Link workers are professionals who reach out from their particular discipline such as a teacher or social worker and link with other teams to share their expertise. But the discourse on exclusion takes place among a select population of professionals and those liable to be excluded are not usually privy to the discourse arenas, literature, conferences, decision making processes or the mechanisms for categorising pupils.

Aiming High: Raising the Achievement of Ethnic Minority Pupils and *Every Child Matters* were published by the DfEE in 2003, after the death of Victoria Climbié, an African child who died despite repeated reports to Social Services. They highlight issues that affect the lives of young people who may be considered at greater risk of exclusion because of their ethnic origin, are in care or have special needs. *Aiming High* identified the characteristics of a successful school as one that has strong leadership, high expectations, effective teaching and learning, an ethos of respect and parental involvement. *Aiming High* discussed how money should be spent to raise achievement of Caribbean African young people. It put into place a multi-layered programme of activities including specialist training for senior school staff planned through the National College for School Leadership. The Black Pupils Achievement Programme is now part of the National Strategies.

Exclusion was identified as a key issue of concern as African pupils were found to be three times more likely to be excluded compared to white pupils. Under the Race Relations (Amendment) Act 2000, schools have to explain such discrimination.

Money influences the decisions about education provision. Viewing education as a commodity has created notions of a purchaser with the ability to purchase an education. Schools have to market themselves with glossy brochures and they work hard to protect their reputation as reflected through examination league tables (Bourne, 1994). League tables can render a school attractive to parents. But it can also cause schools to reject children who they fear may bring them down in the league tables.

> Institutional racism in schools and the education system is a cause of the exclusions gap ... decisions made by people, who themselves may not be consciously racist, have the unintentional and cumulative effect of producing a racist outcome (one that has a disproportionately negative impact on one or more ethnic groups). (DfES, 2006)

The government and the research community are largely preoccupied with harvesting statistics. But as this book argues, this scarcely takes us anywhere towards social inclusion. Most of the existing research targets the student as a statistic. It fails to recognise that behaviour is a symptom of an underlying matter and cannot be solved simply by focusing on conflict or anger-management alone (Majors, 2001).

Labels such as 'disaffected' can stigmatise, pathologise and de-humanise students. Teachers can develop low expectations of the academic ability and behaviours of pupils so described and may view them as deviant, culturally deprived and unintelligent.

Yet students don't make unreasonable demands. One young delegate to a conference in the London Borough of Ealing in 2004 on Collaboration and Change spoke for many when stating:

> We would like schools to make sure that we are treated fairly in school instead of [them] constantly underestimating us.

School practice

Worryingly, a review of the literature found no significant UK research that targets the inclusive practitioner as a key informant. Instead, the UK research community has tended to attribute school exclusions to a child-focused special education needs, behaviour, language or race issue. Whereas I have sought to place the behaviour of the practitioner and the voice of the marginalised in a central position.

The conventional construction of teachers is linked to school-based teaching practice and curriculum delivery and more recently to delivery of the national curriculum. Practitioners are told what to do but rarely how to do it. Teachers are expected to become inclusive practitioners, but what distinguishes an inclusion practitioner from an ordinary teacher?

Although the National Curriculum 2000 includes a statutory inclusion statement that makes it clear that *schools have responsibility to provide a broad and balanced curriculum for all pupils* (DfEE, 1999); issues of humanity and personal growth can be neglected by overworked or incompetent professionals. Often recognition of a child's spiritual, cultural and identity needs is overlooked despite the three principles for inclusion set out in the National Curriculum.

The National Curriculum inclusion statement (1999) requires teachers to have due regard to the following principles when setting suitable learning challenges:

1. Teachers should aim to give every pupil the opportunity to experience success in learning and to achieve as high a standard as possible. The National Curriculum programmes of study set out what most pupils should be taught at each key stage – but teachers should teach the knowledge, skills and understanding in ways that suit their pupils abilities. This may mean choosing knowledge, skills and understanding from earlier or later key stages so that individual pupils can make progress and show what they can achieve. Where it is appropriate for pupils to make extensive use of content from an earlier key stage, there may not be time to teach all aspects of the age-related programmes of study. A similarly flexible approach will be needed to take account of any gaps in pupils learning resulting from missed or interrupted schooling [for example, that may be experienced by travellers, refugees, those in care or those with long-term medical conditions, including pupils with neurological problems, such as head injuries and those with degenerative conditions].

2. For pupils whose attainments fall significantly below the expected levels at a particular key stage, a much greater degree of differentiation will be necessary. In these circumstances, teachers may need to use the content of the programmes of study as a resource or to provide a context, in planning learning appropriate to the age and requirements of their pupils.

3. For pupils whose attainments significantly exceed the expected level of attainment within one or more subjects during a particular key stage, teachers will need to plan suitably challenging work. As well as drawing on materials from later key stages or higher levels of study, teachers may plan further differentiation by extending the breadth and depth of study within individual subjects or by planning work, which draws on the content of different subjects. (Qualifications and Curriculum Authority, 2007)

The government has directed the setting up of multi-professional teams designed to support primary and secondary schools to develop whole school approaches in the areas of promoting positive behaviour and emotional well-being. Many different types of organisations are being funded to address the increasing disaffection which is affecting young people. Connexions, is one such government-funded service offering advice, guidance and careers information through teams of personal advisors who work with young people aged 13 to 19. The objective of social inclusion practice is essentially to engage disengaged young people in education or employment.

Inclusion recognises the education environmental causation of under-achievement (Ryan, 1976). This entails reforming school values and practices so as to make schools more responsive in terms of valuing diversity of gender, nationality, race, language, social background, educational achievement and disability. The term inclusion helps teachers to acknowledge the shared responsibility of failing young people and to develop professional practice to assist the learning of all young people (Mittler, 2000).

Including parents and carers

The Plowden report (DfES, 1967) suggested that schools should follow a 12-step programme to involve parents which included a welcoming system, a profile on each child, twice yearly consultation, termly class meetings and a parents association, plus home-visiting in exceptional circumstances (Macbeth, 1993).

Parents may not be aware of these recommendations or the nature of their roles, responsibilities and rights. Having the information would empower them and encourage constructive dialogue. Parents do not know that they are not obligated to send their children to school but are simply required by the local authority to provide evidence that the requirements of full time education are being met (Gold, 2002). However, when a child is in school education and on the register, failure to comply with the attendance requirement becomes a criminal offence.

At the London Schools and the Black Child Conferences in 2002 and 2004 it emerged that African parents do not always know about new concepts and policies that are introduced in education and the jargon loaded discourse may exclude parents who are genuinely trying to work with the school system. For example, special schools were miscon-strued to be places where their children would receive special academic attention. Parents were not aware that children would probably not receive academic input equal to that in mainstream schools (Dhondy, 1985).

No-one is sure how many education projects operate in the UK. Many of those funded by European Social Funds (ESF) go some way to meeting the needs of young people who are at risk of exclusion or excluded. The number is unclear because unlike PRUs, inclusive practice projects are not regulated by the DfES. Like schools, community projects do not exist in a void or operate in isolation but unlike schools they may be funded by outside stakeholders such as charities or lottery funding. Yet not much is known about what constitutes a socially inclusive project approach or what is considered to be social inclusion practice, or whether a model of inclusion within social contexts exist.

2

Marginalised and disaffected children

The journey from childhood to adulthood is processed through school and, sadly this can be racialised leading to marginalisation and exclusion. (Sewell, 1997)

Africans are not a homogenous group and neither are Europeans. Even those loosely categorised as unplaced, excluded, at risk of exclusion and disaffected are individuals with different life experiences, backgrounds and abilities. But what the children of this community share are differential educational provision to the rest of the school population, and certain damaging experiences, which I outline below.

Although research shows that white working class boys are also underachieving, all the research has established that Caribbean African young people, particularly boys, are being failed by the education system, are at greater risk of exclusion and have been consistently so for longer than any other group. They have now become the parents of the group most vulnerable which is a double vulnerability because it places this community at a serious disadvantage in terms of employability, health, education and housing. Government statistics indicate that poverty is a trap for people who do not have the means to escape through employment or education opportunities and the mortality rate through poor health, drugs, gun violence, gangs, unwanted pregnancy, homelessness, low self-esteem, depression and despair can impact disproportionately on young people pathologised and excluded from school and society.

Blanket definitions do not properly reflect the varied experiences of young people and their families. Inclusive practices operate in a way that respects and value the perspective, culture, heritage and experiences of young people and their families. Professionals have to work to reduce any tendencies to be biased and commit to engaging with communities, even if this entails ongoing dialogue about institutional racism and the disproportionate exclusion of certain students. I call these thorny discussions difficult conversations. During this sensitive process it is unhelpful to categorise, label or pathologise a young person.

Enduring post-colonial trauma

My data showed that school has become a place for enduring psychological trauma for thousands of young people and their families. Parents speak of their fear for their child's future or are afraid that their child is being victimised because they intervened at school. It is not unlike the periods of enslavement and colonial rule where parents justifiably feared for the safety and future of their children.

As a result of negative school experiences, young people and the communities they come from, through no fault of their own, may become

- linguistically compromised
- culturally deficient
- emotionally depressed
- physically insecure
- Psychologically confused and philosophically estranged
- spiritually inadequate

This chapter goes on to discuss each of these issues.

Linguistic compromise

One consequence of being born an African in the Diaspora is that English is the only language of communication. This can create a linguistic challenge that prevents Africans from communicating how desperately exclusion affects them. The extent and nature of the impact on marginalised communities of school exclusion is under-researched. I have witnessed people stutter and suppress their emotions as they search for words to convey the enormity of their negative school experience.

Adults who were traumatised by their school experience struggled and in many instances could not articulate what had happened to them in an unemotional and coherent way. People spoke of feeling disadvantaged and inadequate, afraid of choosing the wrong words to express what they mean. I was repeatedly told that they cannot communicate precisely what they mean without appearing aggressive or clumsy, so ultimately they stopped trying. As they cannot verbally defend their children or themselves frustration builds up.

Many people in this study conveyed a dread of speaking in public because they worry that they will experience the humiliation they endured at school when they used the wrong words to say what they meant. Despite being fluent in colloquial languages from their community such as patois, or in the case of white working-class and British born people of Caribbean African heritage, cockney rhyme and slang. Because these linguistic forms were frowned upon they found it difficult to be heard in European paradigmatic spaces. Yet in culturally sensitive spaces the most inarticulate became the most articulate with what William Henry calls a commonly agreed language (2006).

> *We are reclaiming a healthy lifestyle and rejecting everything that is harmful to us including mainstream school. We home school and are re-languaging. For instance we have renamed the eighth month of the year Mosiah after Marcus Mosiah Garvey who inspires us instead of August which is named after a historical oppressor Augustus Caesar.* (Caribbean African community *Mwalimu* (Kiswahili for cultural teacher))

Many excluded young people nest in their bedrooms for hours, watching TV, texting on their mobile phones or engaging with virtual friends on the internet. They use cyber talk and street talk, coupled with a new *blinglish* language of hidden meanings in fast RAP (rhythm and poetry) music to communicate as well as gain peer acceptance and status for their skill of language creation and reformation. The form fuses art, expression and life in what Gilroy describes as the qualities of an African legacy (2006). A cultural form which has its origins in Jamaica exploded in the UK in the 1970s and existed in reggae-dancehalls, permitting a hidden voice to be heard and allowing young people to speak across geographical borders in a way that was representative of a lived blak reality (Henry, 2006). Young people continue to gain acceptance on their own terms with lyrics they spit (chat) on the mic.

They communicate in spaces they have created for themselves where there is little adult restriction such as email, internet chatrooms, myspace.com, street talk, web-based forums, college canteens, fast food restaurants, playgrounds, illegal radio stations, virtual flyposting sites, other internet forums and poetry circuits. The language is new, abbreviated, reconstructed and reversed. Four or five years ago, baaaad meant very good indeed. Now the word sick has replaced baaaad; shower means great or number one top dawg; friends are called bredrens; slippin means lowered standards. Mobile phones, text language and the language of the internet chatrooms are many young people's lifeline.

> *My mum took my mobile phone and so I was gonna leave home. She ain't got no right to do that. You get me!* (10 year-old boy)

Cultural deficit

Cultural heritage is a source of strength and pride that aids self-confidence and learning. Young people need a strong sense of identity and cultural awareness, but this is difficult when the image of Africa and Africans portrayed in the media holds little appeal for African children in the UK (Nantambu, 1996).

> *We don't buy into the idea that our children are our friends. Children are children and we are the parents they must know that. These notions of buying our children's friendship is rubbish. Todays parents are different they gave the government too much power. My parents didn't care what was happening in my friends house I couldn't come with no disrespect ... they wasn't having none of it.* (Caribbean African parent)

Young British born African people have a cultural birthright from Africa through the Caribbean. The notion that the history of African people begins with the period of enslavement is misguided. But children of mixed and Caribbean African heritage born into western societies often lack the knowledge which their relatives who were born in or still live in the original cultural communities take for granted. Most parents expose their children to culturally sensitive experiences, thus showing them that theirs is a rich cultural birthright passed down through the generations and successfully transfer culture. But others who have worked hard to assimilate into British culture may have left the Caribbean African culture bequeathed to them behind. So they cannot give their children sufficient cultural grounding to help them resist a growing street culture. Young people may consequently feel culturally inadequate and gravitate toward belonging to a pseudo family, peers they can identify with outside of their home and school such as gangs, and thus counteract exclusion from society.

The ripple effect of exclusion has huge implications for society in producing a generation of disaffected and disconnected young adults who are traumatised, misunderstood, poverty stricken and frustrated and without the currency in the form of educational qualifications to enter a society that places greater value on economics and material wealth than on people. This is compounded by media stereotypes that popularise pseudo-American street cultures – the music videos and programmes that portray African American culture as all about guns and gansta rap and all people in Africa itself as malnourished and dependent on charity. Alternative frames of reference, such as cultural rites of passage or traditional teachings, have largely been replaced in the minds of children by the media images.

> *Adults don't even look us in the eyes no more. We are targets and suspects all at the same time.* (British born African adolescent)

Pupils and their families from various ethnic groups may have different frames of reference and face structural barriers to achievement. Accordingly, practitioners need a range of skills that go beyond subject specialisms (Piggott, 1995). Later chapters describe the range of skills extending beyond the curriculum specialisms and customary school pedagogy generally taught to teachers.

Emotional depression

The expression of emotion is partly culturally determined so can be easily misunderstood. Laughing – which mask deep anxiety is often misconstrued by teachers as defiance or bravado; smiling at irony misinterpreted as smirking; shaking your head in disbelief as refusal to communicate. My research discovered that young people are responding to scenarios inappropriately and any frustration or embarrassment they may express in a way that does not immediately convey remorse is frowned upon by teachers.

The data showed that teachers become uncomfortable, flustered, flushed and tearful when parents raise issues of unfair treatment or excessive punishment. These teachers continue to pathologise and threaten students with exclusion whilst parents are left reluctant to express their concern. Practitioners sometimes appear to lack appropriate emotion when communicating with parents about children's achievement or the challenges they present. Research indicates that there is a need for professionals to develop emotional literacy and empathy (Majors, 2001).

> It is time for us to reclaim our children. If teachers cared, they would show it. We need to educate them ourselves because we don't want to explain anymore. (African Community Activist)

My research indicates that parents have more confidence in a teacher who expresses empathy, interest and compassion and who can discuss sensitive issues without becoming defensive or feeling accused. This will strengthen the lines of communication if strategies for achievement are discussed. But too often parents report that some teachers go into emotional meltdown and this interferes with their ability to listen to what the marginalised is saying and learn about their community. A gulf develops, with teachers presuming the concern is about them, their reputation and their career. There needs to be a paradigm shift away from blame, toward solutions which consider more than the here and now and appreciate the journey of the community over recent, historical and Ancestral time.

Parents speak of the inhumanity they perceive in how they are treated, often when they are simply in need of information or a chance to support their child in remaining in school and being included. They express their fear at being accused of being aggressive, arrested and sectioned for mental instability. Parents report that some schools frown upon outward signs of affection or exuberance. Some relate how when they travel to the Caribbean or Africa they encounter remarks about how offspring born and conditioned in the UK to the British stiff upper lip don't know how to relax properly, let their hair down and have a good time.

Insecurity about self image
The western portrayal of beauty does not embrace the dark skin, tight curly or kinky hair, wide nose, generous lips, broad hips and full figure which are features of African and Caribbean perceptions of attractive-

ness. Consequently, young Caribbean Africans may not embrace their own beauty and practitioners who are culturally naïve cannot help young people to develop self-confidence and navigate through an environment that renders young people invisible in media portrayal of beauty. This said, it is still far easer for girls with a smile or coy demeanour to access environments in ways that boys cannot. Boys report that if they smile they are perceived as silly and if they don't they are perceived as aggressive.

Students may engage in harmful eating practices in an attempt to conform to western notions of beauty. The students who have more European features are chosen for prime parts in school productions, publications and other displays in school environments.

> We never got chosen to be the mother of the baby Jesus and teachers were generally less tolerant of us. I couldn't wait to get out. (Caribbean African grandparent)

The media reinforce European notions of beauty, when they should accept and celebrate all natural God-given attributes.

Psychological confusion and philosophical estrangement

The linked histories of Europe and Africa and indeed America have not been truthfully conveyed in school curricula. In history lessons Africans may still be portrayed overtly and covertly as being of the lowest human order, malnourished, diseased, needy recipients of charitable organisations. This causes students to distance themselves from anything African, even their heritage and become philosophically estranged and psychologically confused.

> I didn't like history. I wasn't interested in the Saxons, Romans or Tudors and I learned that African history began with slavery. (Caribbean African parent)

Similar misunderstandings may arise with new arrivals in schools. The countries they come from have different cultural experiences and expectations. Some children may never have received formal education. Some new arrivals may have been subjected to war, trauma and other oppression that has left them ill-equipped to employ appropriate behaviour and psychological responses. Their coping mechanisms and appropriate psychological, emotional and behavioural responses may be underdeveloped.

When young people arrive in the UK they are inserted into the British education system according to their age. Community-focused initiatives provide an education programme for Year 11 refugee students who cannot get into schools. Some community projects will also provide education programmes for students for whom English is not their first language or whose religious practice determines that they should be educated in faith schools or for those who simply cannot get into schools.

Inclusive practice supports these new arrivals' coping ability, orientates and validates their experience, provides a safe learning space and introduces them to other services. Their parents need to know about the British education system because in other countries the responsibility for children's education may rest solely with the teachers.

Spiritual repression

Religion has always been pre-occupied with inclusive and excluding practices. For instance, Catholics were exiled (excluded) to other regions or countries – where they established colleges that combined secondary with university education. Also the church was supportive of the ill treatment of people and condoned the transatlantic trade in Africans. The church has now apologised for the role it played but interestingly the Church of England synod stopped short of endorsing a specific call for reparations despite receiving compensation for the loss of forced African labour on the first Caribbean plantation, Codrington in Barbados.

The *Guardian* reported that on 9 February 2006, Archbishop Rowan Williams told the Synod that the church ought to acknowledge its corporate and ancestral guilt:

> The Body of Christ is not just a body that exists at any one time; it exists across history and we therefore share the shame and the sinfulness of our predecessors and part of what we can do, with them and for them in the Body of Christ, is prayerful acknowledgment of the failure that is part of us, not just of some distant them. To speak here of repentance and apology is not words alone; it is part of our witness to the Gospel, to a world that needs to hear that the past must be faced and healed and cannot be ignored ... by doing so we are actually discharging our responsibility to preach good news, not simply to look backwards in awkward-

ness and embarrassment, but to speak of the freedom we are given to face ourselves, including the unacceptable regions of ... our history.
http://educationforum.ipbhost.com/index.php?showtopic=6093
http://www.guardian.co.uk/religion/Story/0,,1705628,00.html

My experience of anything spiritual in school was conveyed through my Christian schooling, church, hymns and biblical reading. The focus was on religion and images of a blonde-haired blue-eyed Christ were portrayed in almost every religious book I read. I was not told that the original Christian orthodoxy originated in Ethiopia. I was taught to call Jesus Christ the son of the father but it was difficult to reconcile the evident physical differences between myself as an African and Jesus as a Caucasian so I could not see him as my brother or father. Powerful depictions of God and Jesus as a white European, divine, good, master and dark-skinned Africans as the opposite: devilish, cursed, bad and subservient slaves made me uncomfortable.

I recall being bombarded by these images at school, at home, in church, by the media, in publications including the bible but this did not answer my questions. I could not make sense in my mind and heart of the images of unnecessary poverty of people who looked like me. Despite attending a church school, Sunday school and being a devout member of the church choir, this barrier remained and led me to embrace spirituality as a wider holistic concept. This early experience influenced the choices I made later for how worldviews and voices should be permitted to be expressed.

The voices heard in my research are anguished. They reflect the perspectives of professionals, practitioners and young people and their families and indicate the differences in perception among them about education, school services, systems and other matters. The themes that emerged have aided me in mapping a framework of inclusive practice.

Denied histories, discarded cultures – disaffected people

To understand the deep rooted nature of the hurt we must remember that modern forms of thought about society are rooted in the sixteenth and seventeenth century but received their most effective expression in the mid-eighteenth century, the period of Kant's 'Enlightenment' (Hall, 1992).

This period of Enlightenment had a significant impact on the concept of school.

Philosophers and historians shape the documenting of historical events from within their particular frame of reference. Philosophers are influenced by the social climate that they live in and it follows that the work of philosophers and researchers directly and indirectly influenced teaching and learning systems then as they do today.

The histories of Europe and Africa are intertwined (Stokes, 2003; Ashby, 2003) over several centuries and are significant in terms of notions of mainstream and inclusion. That Africa influenced Greece is irrefutable.

The way that history has been taught in UK schools is that the ancient history of Europe was linked to Greece. What was omitted was that the ancient history of Africa is inextricably linked to Kemet (Ancient Egypt) (Diop, 1978). World histories have been excluded in Europe's school curriculum portrayal of history along with the philosophies of excluded people and their corresponding social customs.

The exclusion of histories and historical events prevents a holistic perspective necessary in a contemporary Europe which has its roots in a history that is intertwined with the histories of other peoples who make up the modern diverse population (Diop, 1978).

The period of Enlightenment still underpins the social sciences today (Hall, 1992). It's philosophies influence policy and form the backdrop to behaviours and practice that take place inside schools and inform the decision-making processes that lead to the alarming number of Caribbean African children being excluded today.

There are, however American African philosophers. Molefi Kete Asante introduces notions of being and knowing which extend beyond the Enlightenment. Asante (1988) argues that the special role history assigns to the scholar can be elusive and uncomfortable and that there is no way to talk about education without looking again at the roots of world history and the interplay of the histories of various people. Consequently scholars such as myself have a duty to endure occasional discomfort and be both persistent and resilient in the pursuit of new understandings. Indeed it is the researcher who is often the first to discover and present new knowledge pleasant or unpleasant.

We suggest that deconstruction can help us to read policy documents around their own blind spot and to disrupt their own decidability. Analysis of this kind positions the researcher as a kind of cultural vigilante seeking to expose exclusion in all its forms, the language we use, the teaching methods we adopt, the curriculum we transmit and the relationships we establish within our schools. (Slee and Allan, 2001)

Philosophy and process

During Europe's philosophical period of Enlightenment, Africans were considered to be only three fifths human and even referred to as the noble savage in certain circles. The remnants of this practice could be said to form the justification for the unequal treatment of certain groups to this day and may form the largely sub conscious basis of continued unfair treatment of Africans who include Caribbean and British Africans.

Philosopher Cheikh Anta Diop (1978) considers it critical to know one's self but also asserts the importance of knowing one's cultural origin, history and difference by promoting the concept of African identity.

In the 1960s and 1970s the influence of America on Africans was powerful with the civil rights movements and the struggle for integration. Until then Africans in the US were not entitled to attend the same schools as their white counterparts. During the period of African enslavement, Africans were downgraded to being property or chattels, to be bought or discarded, as the owner saw fit.

Under the Three-Fifths Compromise in the US Constitution (1787) enslaved Africans were counted as three-fifths of a human being for the purpose of determining a state's representation in Congress. Article 1, Section 2, Clause 3 of the constitution explains the apportionment of representation and taxation. It reads:

Representatives and direct taxes shall be apportioned among the several States which may be included within this Union, according to their respective numbers, which shall be determined by adding to the whole number of free Persons, including those bound to Service for a Term of Years and excluding Indians not taxed, three fifths of all other Persons.

31

This clause is often singled out today as a sign of African dehumanisation to three-fifths human because at the time the clause was generated, enslaved people in America were dark-skinned Africans.

Chattel slavery was also prominent in the Caribbean. The consequences of this were and remain psychologically devastating for people from this community.

Enslavement persists in many forms in many parts of the world. However, the barbaric treatment of Africans in economic trade resulted in enslaved Africans being reduced to no more than objects of possession or chattels in a way no other peoples have endured.

Colonised Africans were given names with colonial links instead of the authentic symbolic meanings of traditional African cultures. Caribbean Africans can be linked back to the people who brutalised and enslaved their Africans Ancestors and imposed plantation holder names on them.

In Africa, names and naming ceremonies are important. Traditionally, names had tribal or cultural significance that conveyed a certain perceived energy, purpose or personality. Now many diasporan Africans have sir names (surnames) that serve to remind them of an abhorrent period in history and keep alive the names of plantation owners and enslavers. Many children of African and Caribbean African origin have Christian first names such as Mary or popular culture names such as Keisha and Shaneiqua, that have no traditional cultural meaning but instead link to modern day media celebrities. They may even have names that refer to material wealth or are considered to be fashionable. These names may be linked to transferred aspirations for symbols of success such as Chardonnay, Lexus, Mercedes and Porche. Modern Africanists now take African names or allow names to be chosen for them by Africans with the authority to bestow tribal names. This is as a way to claim their African heritage. This can cause some conflict within diasporan families as parents subjected to colonialisation may feel rejected when their children claim an Ancestral name that they prefer to answer to.

There are thousands of people of Caribbean African origin who are unable to construct a generational family tree because the shared histories are kept secret.

This undermines the historical link to their positive African heritage. Indeed even some descendants of Africans who remained on the continent distanced themselves from Caribbean Africans.

> *Africans used to call us names like slave babies and we called them derogatory names too. We have been called all sorts like BOAC children because some of us came here in the 70s on BOAC planes.* (Caribbean African)

The dehumanising avoidance of naming Africans correctly is consistent through various British historical periods. Nothing is said of the African presence being a strong one, reflected, for instance, in European culture with the presence of the Moors in Elizabethan theatre evidenced by blacking-up (Walker, 2006).

When the perception revealed in the voices of this qualitative research is combined with the statistical data from quantitative research, a disturbing picture emerges of the lived experience of the African in the Caribbean, America and Britain.

The causes are complex but the media exerts huge influence. Subliminal messages in media and music continue to influence the views of young people who aspire to look and be like their music icons and role models.

> One of the enduring legacies of the *MA'AFA* (Kiswahili word which means great disaster and terrible loss usually referred to as the transatlantic slave trade) is the perpetuation of a colour caste system institutionalised during African enslavement. The British Empire used divide and rule strategy to create factions in unified groups by deliberately giving preferential treatment to one group based on superficial differences. Lighter skinned African people, or indeed the dual heritage children born as a result of the extensive and systematic rape by slavers of African women who were often afforded marginally better treatment at the hands of their enslavers.

> The residual outcome of this is present in the western media where African women such as the music entertainer Beyonce are presented as a light skinned, blond woman to promote a cultural aesthetic which is anti-African whilst the successful African entertainer, Michael Jackson, uses chemical agents and invasive surgical operations to entirely suppress all vestiges of his African identity.

In 1999, politician Jeffery Archer received wide-scale condemnation after he announced: Your head did not turn in the road if a black woman passed because they were badly dressed, probably overweight and probably had a lousy job. If you walk down London streets now there are most staggeringly beautiful girls of every nationality. That is part of getting rid of prejudice and making things equal,

The attack on the African aesthetic is unrelenting and we must therefore ensure that our defence is holistic and wide-ranging. (www.ligali.org.uk)

Many of my respondents speak of being unable to reconcile the history they were given in school with the history they discovered when they got older. As a child I recall that the map of Great Britain in my primary classroom looked some ten times bigger than Africa. I did not know that Britain was a country and Africa was a vast continent. I did not know that the so called transatlantic slave trade was an African genocide, a period of enslavement, imperialism, colonialism, invasions, oppression and exploitation of millions of Africans, not the respectable trade I was led to believe it was.

...never would we forget
the abhorrent atrocities our ancestors met
and always would we remember with pride
in spirit of the African genocide
that our cultural legacies positively exist for ever
(Grace Quansah, 2007)

Reading widely after school, studying the messages in reggae music and hearing stories from the mouths of African and Caribbean African storytellers, social commentators (*Jeli, Jali, Gewal, Gawlo* or *Griots* – West African terms for keepers of knowledge) and the quietly patient nuances and wisdom of elders stories, I learned of other more appropriate non-English words like *Shoah* (Hebrew) used to describe the devastation wrought by the Nazi Holocaust and *MA'AFA* regarding the African holocaust.

The way we see it

Young people survive by being bicultural so that they can comply with the wishes of adults without selling out themselves or each other. They live in a wider society than school and family and operate in a hidden youth culture of their own – in effect a sub society. This biculturalism equips them to counteract the effects of this enduring stress and some students become

- proactive, by working to prevent the impact of stressful situations and allow people to make judgements. Some will work hard to surprise teachers and parents who have low expectations

- reactive, trying to minimise the impact on them of enduringly stressful situations in school and backchat (talk back to teachers)

- passive in their response to the enduring stress of a negative environment with emotional numbness or ignorance, for instance being resigned to let teachers do and say what they like because there doesn't seem to be any point in resisting

Young people are not oblivious to their under-achievement and have ideas about how their school careers could be more successful. They are frank and recognise that it is not all their fault but that they can play a part in making things better.

This chapter ends with telling quotes from my interviewees. They are just a sample of responses from the data. As I proceeded to chart the research approach, I knew it had to be guided by the voices and views of those I was researching.

Children age 7 to 11

I asked children what could be done to improve their chances of staying in school and doing better in class. These were some of the replies:

If no one talked in class, I could listen to the teacher and learn better.

If I get more sleep, I would be early for school.

The teacher doesn't like me and when I put my hand up she tells me to put it down.

The teacher should not shout and tell us not to shout.

My mum and dad argue a lot and I can't sleep.

I get bullied all the time but teachers don't care.

I try to ignore people when they are in trouble so that I don't get into trouble.

I go online a lot in my room. Chat rooms are the best or MSN.

I keep being put in the naughty corner, it's not fair.

I like my class and never get told off.

I am early if I run to school.

If I sit by myself I get my work done sometimes.

If I get bored, I text my friends and they text me. The teacher doesn't even notice.

I like it more when the lesson is more interesting.

If I am organised and ignore other people I can finish my work but the teacher keeps putting noisy children near me.

I need help but my helper is not always there.

When I leave school I'm gonna be a music producer, I already make beats.

Adolescents age 12 to 17

Young people were asked to share their experiences of high school and say what they really thought.

Teachers used to dash us out of the room and we had to go to the divisional head. In our school they had a plain whitewashed room with a peephole and a table and one chair. They made us sit in the room without any work. They tried to isolate to control, but it ended up just being a treat for us. They should have dealt with the matter at the time instead it rolled over to the next lesson with that teacher. (Ex-pupil)

There is evidence to suggest that inclusive practice intervention has a positive impact in terms of preventing exclusions. This is what a number of young people said about themselves

Once my teacher listened to me, I realised that I could not understand before. Now I'm gonna go to college and do I.T. I wanna teach when I get my qualifications

I was getting into fights ... now I graduated ahead of others. I think that it's important that this (social inclusion) project carries on because I know there is a lot of kids out there who are just lost. They need some form of direction if they don't have that kind of direction they can go into the bad zone... whatever that may be on the streets.

I was gonna write some letters but it's really hard to explain how it helps.

They helped me get into college and helped me with problems at home as well.

I realise like, they done it so that you had other people in your school that you could relate to. Like they knew ... Met ... got on with. So, when you're in school sort of – when I was at school, I only spoke to one person because I was never there. So, I only went there and saw him and spoke to him and when he was like ... left school, went to lessons and just ... stuff like.

But then when I meet them they sort of – they used to come up to me and say, hi and stuff. You know, just for that year. It made me want to go to school more because I know more people, sort of.

This (social inclusion) project puts you onto the point where you're thinking for yourself. You're responsible for your own actions, which is important you know, teenagers or even kids, or sometimes even adults, you know.

I'm now in College. I've actually finished my national diploma in performing arts. I passed as well. I found out yesterday. I'm quite happy about that. And, I couldn't do that without them (community-based project) either. So I'm quite happy. And, I'm actually now taking an apprenticeship in business of arts administration.

They've helped me out in quite a lot of problems as well.

Parents

Parents were asked to say what they felt about under-achievement and school exclusions.

They keep changing the teachers so what's the point.

I didn't get my qualifications so I hope my children do.

Just because we're black it doesn't mean we are all the same.

Teachers are arrogant, so I'm just waiting till my son leaves that school.

I can't let the school know that her father has left, I know what they're like.

Teachers

Teachers were asked about their view on raising achievement and school exclusions. Some of the responses were:

> We can't let one child disrupt the whole class, so I will exclude any child. If they happen to be black that doesn't make me racist.

> I won't tolerate anyone shouting at me.

> Parents don't show an interest and they never show up at parents evening.

> If they don't want to learn, that's up to them.

> You don't know what it's like to teach a class of 30 children.

Behaviour needs to be linked to voices, views and what is happening in a wider social context and what is going on in the world of the child (Gold, 2002).

3

Pathologising vulnerable children

Children are in emergency mode, seeking our help. A young person's first line of defence is their own moral compass. As adults we must intercede to stop losing tomorrow's leaders to drugs, delinquency and teenage pregnancy. (Rites of Passage Elder Emily Gunter, USA)

Vulnerable populations

In its inaugural report *Truancy and School Exclusion* (1998b), the Social Exclusion Unit identified the young people most vulnerable to exclusion:

- Travellers
- Caribbean African boys
- high mobility pupils
- white working-class boys
- young offenders
- pregnant teenagers
- children with medical needs
- children educated other than at school
- refugees/asylum seekers
- looked after children (children in care of social services)
- children without a school place
- excluded pupils
- Pupil Referral Unit pupils

The differentiation of young people into these vulnerable groups marginalises many of them. Issues are imposed upon them about either not belonging or belonging. Some young people may belong to more than one vulnerable group, further marginalising and disadvantaging them.

Fifty per cent of excluded young people were in education, training or employment up to two years after their permanent exclusion from mainstream school (Daniels and Sellman, 2003). So half were not. They were unplaced in education and unplaced in employment. And research (eg. Dhondy 1985) indicates that unplaced young people end up at the bottom of the British ladder of labour unless they are reintegrated into education or employment.

Martin Narey, Director General of HM Prison Service notes the connection between young people who are excluded from school and the criminal justice system. My research indicates that a person's self esteem is affected and that if aspirations are not realised, depression looms. They can feel resentment and anger when they realise that their school experience was abusive and unjust.

When one looks at the treatment of African patients in mental health care and the disproportionate sectioning of Africans (44% higher than for white people, according to the The 1990 Trust, 2006), plus the disproportionate policing and punishment of African offenders, it seems hard to believe that the education, health and justice services deliver equally to all Britain's citizens.

Yet the cost of differential treatment is immense for the justice system and for mental and health services. So is the expense of consequent unemployment benefit, anti-social behaviour orders and crime. The loss to society of the knowledge and skills of marginalised people is tragic.

Currently, the response to the disaffection and disengagement of young people in the education system has been in the form of raising achievement and widening participation such as through the DfES Aiming Higher programme. Closer scrutiny is needed of institutional structures, individual practices and educational processes that result in differential treatment of certain sectors of the school population (Gillborn, 1987; Gillborn and Mirza, 2000; Rassool and Morley, 2000).

Because of the denial of shared histories, African children lose out on schooling and endure the emotional and social consequences which rebound on to the individual, their families, communities and wider society. We must recognise these shared histories and use them to gain deeper understanding and learn lessons. We must care enough to overcome the discomfort of looking at all the possible reasons why we are faced with such appalling exclusion statistics.

The early historical context

As far back as the 1700s education providers considered many children to be educationally subnormal and even ineducable. This widespread and acceptable practice contrasts with the words of the Secretary of State for Education in 2004, who asserted that

> Children who are treated as though they are ineducable almost invariably become ineducable.

During African enslavement and British colonial rule, European girls and women could accuse the Africans of any crime without having to prove it. The men could even be executed. A delegate at a recent conference, 'In God's Name? The role of the Church in the Transatlantic Slave Trade' suggested that nothing has changed, citing state schools and church schools are equally culpable of pathologising African boys.

This young British born Caribbean African man maintained that:

> *White teachers are scared of us so how can they discipline us fairly. Young people are just simply trying to receive the respect and justice we were never shown in school. You got to understand the situation we live in, it's deeper than just carrying a weapon. Kids won't turn to police nah, rather talk to older cousin for justice. They (police) always arrest us, that's just straight. Incidents happen on the bus, on the street and the police don't wanna get involved until after something has happened*

My research shows that parents feel guilty for allowing the teaching profession, which is dominated by European women, to exclude or cause their children to be excluded from school. Many are aware that a disproportionate number are Caribbean African boys.

We have seen how special education became a feature of public education in the UK, and considered the more recent rhetoric of inclusive education. However the concept of inclusiveness is not new. To explain the concept of inclusion, I distinguish between social movement concerned with structural problems in society and historical movement over a period (Delanty, 1999). If we look at the differing expectations we begin to see how the many misunderstandings accumulate.

From the late 1950s through to the '70s there was a large influx of people to the UK from the Caribbean. They had different geographical, social, political, economic, spiritual and cultural backgrounds but all came to work hard and serve in response to the Britain's call for assistance to re-build war-torn England. Their expectations were high and they intended to be here for three to five years at most.

On arrival many of them were met with hostility but still they stayed, worked to rebuild the health service, transport and other areas of the UK's infrastructure. They began to settle, still holding on to the intention to stay for a few years only before returning home to the Caribbean. As time passed they yearned for the families they had left behind and so they sent for them.

Many of the children had been separated from their parents for several years and had formed secure attachments with grandparents, aunts or other entrusted people. When they arrived in the UK some children had difficulty adjusting to a strange environment, re-establishing strained attachments with parents, readjusting emotionally and culturally whilst at the same time grappling with language nuances, teacher attitudes, different expectations and teaching styles.

> *When I arrived from the Jamaica, I was placed in the lower set. My history teacher told me that there is one thing he can't stand more than a nigger and that's a paki. I've never forgotten that and I'm 53.* (Caribbean African parent)

Caribbean African parents were unaware of the overt and covert subtleties of racism and had great respect for and confidence in teachers. They believed everything teachers said even if it was in conflict with the social injustice their child would try to alert them to. This caused great frustration and confusion.

> *They knew we were coming and made no preparation to receive us warmly. What has changed? We came here to help rebuild Great Britain. I'm fed up of it. Lack of history in schools, stop and search on road and the break up of black families. They know what they're doing. It's not an accident, it's by design.* (Caribbean African parent)

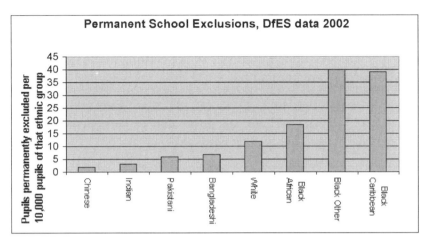

Table 3.1 DfES Permanent School Exclusion 2002 Data Chart

Some teachers abused the parents' trust. Many young people from the Caribbean were disadvantaged by what their teachers did. This placed adult, adolescent and younger African males at a lasting disadvantage, unable to exploit employment and career opportunities because they were not given equal access to education in the UK.

> *I was a high achiever in Barbados but when I went to school here, they asked me where I was from and then put in the lowest set. Every one in my set was black and we were all from the West Indies. We were ignored when we put our hands up in class and I soon learned there was no point learning.* (Caribbean African parent)

The 1944 Education Act never came to terms with the aspirations of Britain's post-war immigrants. The courage and number of African loyalists who fought on the side of the British during the American War for Independence created a large degree of visibility in the UK, yet they were still singled out as constituting a major social problem (Bourne, 1994; Campbell, 1985).

In the Caribbean schools generally have high expectations of their pupils, irrespective of their background. Marginalisation and under-achievement are not a major feature of discussions about educational achievement. Major equality issues of colour, gender, class, disability or other matters like race do not feature in the way they do in the UK. There is no so called fear factor associated with words like 'intimidating', 'disruptive' or 'behavioural' in the way they are associated with African boys and exclusion in the UK.

43

The British education system clearly failed to take on board the needs of these new students who arrived during the late 1950s and 1960s. If students did not respond positively to the existing teaching methods they were considered subnormal and in some cases disruptive.

In the same year Bernard Coard's book appeared Neely Fuller Jr published a little known workbook called *The United Independent Compensatory Code/System/Concept*. In it he stated:

> If you do not understand white supremacy (racism) – what it is and how it works – everything else that you understand, will only confuse you. (Fuller Jr, 1971)

From 1997 to the present

Labour's landslide victories in 1997 and 2001 allowed them to re-formulate policies and win the support of many of the middle-class voters who were disenchanted with Tory politics. In their formulation of policy they included the discourse of inclusion.

The Education department directed local authorities (LEAs) to work towards getting the needs of special education needs students met within mainstream school provision. The strategy was underpinned by the drive for social inclusion. Government-funded initiatives sought to address the issue of school exclusion.

However, the current social inclusion strategy ignores the lived realities of both the excluder and the excluded and merely reports on the conditions and symptoms of exclusion. It fails to include human needs as a strategic education priority and concerns itself mainly with statistics.

The statistics indicate that school exclusion is disproportionately applied to certain sectors of the population:

> Pupils with statements of SEN are much more likely to be excluded from school than those who do not have statements. In 1996/97, 1.11 per cent of all pupils with statements of SEN were excluded from school compared to only 0.14 per cent of the rest of the school population – the former rate being 8 times the latter. (Decrease in 1998/99 – 0.91 per cent pupils with SEN compared 0.11 per cent i.e. just over 7 times).

> Between 1995 and 1999, around 83 per cent of all permanent exclusions were boys.

From 1995/96 to 1997/98, about 27 in every 10,000 boys were excluded, dropping to 22 in every 10,000 in 1998/9; (rates for girls: 6 per 10,000 in 1995/65, 1996/97 and 5 per 10,000 in 1997/98 and 1998/99)

The most common age for exclusion is 14 and altogether nearly 8 out of 10 exclusions are of pupils aged 12-15 just before critical exams.

A higher proportion of black Caribbean, black African and black Other groups were excluded than that of any other ethnic groups. In 1997/98 the rate of exclusion for black Caribbean pupils was 4.5 times more than that for white pupils. (DfEE, 2000)

This chart from the DfES (page 43) illustrates the figures of permanent exclusions of various populations in 2002. Even at first glance the disparity is alarming. On further examination it becomes apparent that the category Black Other which has been created further marginalises and belittles African people. Black Other is likely to comprise the Africans who refuse to be categorised as black Caribbean or black African and might well include students who are dark-skinned but claim no African-related identity.

An Ofsted report (Gillborn and Mirza, 2000) found that:

- African pupils often enter school better prepared than any other group but fall behind as they move through the school system

- The achievement gap between 16 year-old white pupils and their Pakistani and Caribbean African classmates has roughly doubled since the late 1980s

Guidance on planning for inclusion is urgently needed: the government sets no national targets and some LEAs are setting targets that will result in greater inequalities in the future.

The Department for Education (DfEE, 2000; DfEE, 2001) and the Social Exclusion Unit (SEU, 1998b) statistics highlight the over-representation of African boys permanently excluded from school. At a recent conference, Diane Abbott MP described the silent catastrophe of African boys' under-achievement as an issue that no one wants to talk about for fear of being branded as a racist.

African boys in years 10 and 11 experience complex compounded risks of permanent exclusion in addition to gender and race (Gillborn and

Mirza, 2000). Speaking at the London Schools and the Black Child Conference in 2003, David Gillborn said:

> Schools separate children on the basis of perceived ability, aptitude and attitude, thereby institutionalising failure caused by setting by ability (streaming) based on school notions of how clever young people are (expectations).

The pathologisation of African children

For decades the perceived solution to the problem of teaching young people of African and Caribbean African heritage was simply to remove many of them from school. Thousands of young people were excluded from regular classroom situations and sent to education provision for children with perceived lesser educational ability (Coard, 1971). Uninformed, culturally naive school professionals began to pathologise these children, diagnosing them as having special needs and sentencing them to inappropriate and unfulfilling experiences of school because of language prejudice and low teacher expectations. The parents believed that special needs provision was a way of valuing special children. By the time educators, politicians, parents, activists and others became aware of what was happening, the impact of the negative reception into schools had already affected thousands of young people.

Many African parents and grandparents were themselves marginalised or excluded from school, so have never attained positions fitting their intelligence and ability. Some of them have contributed to this research. They express their frustration and disappointment that they have become the disaffected parents of children who are at risk of exclusion and who in turn are becoming disaffected. Because of their own negative school experience some of them cannot offer the support and assistance for their children's education and are reluctant to become involved in the activities which surround and enhance educational achievement.

Thousands of African parents faced poverty as a direct result of their disadvantaged education. School was a traumatic experience for many. They feel robbed of the chance for academic qualifications and the social development and life skills needed to compete in today's global market. They have been left with battered self-esteem, incorrect notions of the contribution their ancestors made to world civilisation and poor self-image – and all because the schools failed them.

46

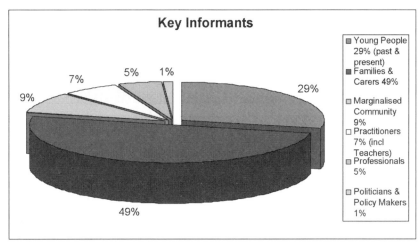

Figure 3.1 Key Informants

I homeschool her now. I had to go to websites and download information about black scientists and inventors. She didn't know that black people invented things, in fact she didn't believe me at first. (Caribbean African parent)

Today African pupils are still disadvantaged, but in more sophisticated ways. For instance many have been unable to secure a school place. If a school declares itself full when a student applies, they become educationally unplaced and socially displaced. This can lead to disaffection, for which they are then blamed and pathologised. A devastating vicious cycle begins with being without a school place, which compounds the disadvantage that can lead to disaffection. Not all parents know how the education admission and exclusion appeals procedure works, so their child remains disadvantaged. A child who cannot get a school place can experience exclusion and lack the support or guidance they so greatly need.

Exclusion and teachers

In 1994 UNESCO (United Nations Educational, Scientific and Cultural Organisation) organised a conference which clarified the philosophy and practice of inclusion. It stated that inclusion and participation are essential to human dignity and to the exercise and enjoyment of human rights. And it stated that human differences are normal and that learning differences must be accommodated by adapting teaching to meet

47

the needs of the child, and urged ordinary schools to recognise and respond to the diverse needs of the students (Mittler, 2000).

Good teachers do not use exclusion as the first form of discipline but work hard to be inclusive practitioners. However, their good work is undermined by colleagues who are comfortable about excluding and at the slightest opportunity will exercise power that may ruin a child's life chances.

A report by David Gillborn on *Race, Ethnicity and Education* (1990) showed that Caribbean African children are more likely to receive reprimands than praise even when praise is due. This is a strong indictment of those in the teaching profession, and it is important to remember that many more teachers do treat pupils fairly.

There is considerable research in the area of exclusion but it does not explore the gulf that exists between inclusive practitioners and the teachers who readily exclude young people. The practices of the teachers who do avoid excluding students are not well researched. More attention needs to be paid to the lived experience and practice of inclusive teachers when they work with pupils who are vulnerable to being unplaced, excluded or at risk of exclusion and to how their practice differs from that of teachers who use the threat of exclusion as a strategy for discipline.

Published research largely favours the convention of focusing on the pupil and there is comparatively little basis for judging the practice of teachers, non-teaching staff and social inclusion practitioners in education. It was this neglected but important area that inspired my research investigation, along with the dearth of research that documents the experience of the excluded children who are now adults.

Looking for solutions

The majority of studies about exclusion investigate the cause of exclusion and the profile of excluded young people. I looked, however, at the solutions to combating social exclusion which lie within the socio-cultural perspectives of marginalised young people and the practitioners who successfully engage with them. My research is based on data of which 29 per cent is provided by young people, 49 per cent by their families, 9 per cent by the communities they come from, 7 per cent by frontline practitioners, 5 per cent by other professionals and 1 per cent from others such as policy makers and academic and journalist writers. These key informants have provided an intriguing but alarming picture of the impact of school exclusion.

In addition to the many interview transcripts, issues and themes emerged from the data collected in field notes, document searches, observations and research journals. Conferences and meetings provided additional information. The research analysis provided evidence of a model of socially inclusive practice in education and draws upon the perspectives given by young people, their families, practitioners and professionals which were witnessed during observations and obtained in interviews.

Behaviour and school exclusion

The statistics suggest that schools have a tendency to use excluding practices disproportionately with certain sectors of the pupil population. Further investigation reveals that exclusions often take place at key points in pupils' academic career such as just before exams, obstructing their gaining academic qualifications. At ages 9 to 11 some children begin to disengage because they become aware they are being treated differently from their white peers and that their teachers have low expectations of them. We see that punitive practicc and policies are not uniformly applied but are applied more stringently to Africans and particularly boys. Young people in this research speak frequently about their wish to be treated with respect and fairness by teachers.

> *I was revising for my exams and the teacher said I did something that I didn't. She called me a liar, I'm not a liar. She stopped me from sitting my exams.* (College student)

Parents openly shared their fears about the possible repercussions on their children if they protest at unfair treatment. So they urge them to endure it, just keep their heads down and stay out of trouble, because they need to gain qualifications. Parents feel guilty about having to send their children into a system that treats them harshly and restricts their life opportunities.

All this creates pressure on children who endure a school experience in which they are permanently subdued. This makes them sensitive to injustice when other children are rewarded for their enthusiasm and inquisitiveness while they are reprimanded for similar exuberance. The child who can maintain a level of self-oppression may make it through the school years without being excluded but this can be at the expense of their inquiring mind and spirit. The child may present later with symptoms of psychological stress such as diminished interest and participation in significant activities, a feeling of detachment or estrangement from others, difficulty concentrating and without any expectation of having a career.

Teachers, non-teaching staff and parents who do not resist the unequal circumstances they create for young people collude with the unkindness of such differential schooling. Parents and teachers share the same duty to accept their responsibility to protect vulnerable children. They must therefore have what may be difficult conversations with each other. For all children to have an equal chance to reach their full potential, as laid out in the Every Child Matters agenda, teachers must confront any tendency in themselves or their colleagues to exploit the option of exclusion. To be silent is to collude with those who discriminate.

Excluding practices trap pupils in poverty, placing them at a disadvantage in the labour market from which they may never recover. Young people often endure situations where they are pushed to breaking point. Often their only respite is during weekends, half-terms and holidays.

Parents, practitioners, politicians and government are united in their belief that it is undesirable to exclude children and that inclusive practice is important in raising the attainment of all young people. Yet the number of exclusions remains high and the number of children affected is masked because it conceals those who are kept on school premises but excluded them from regular lessons. These are hidden exclusions, as they do not appear in statistics.

In addition there are pupils who truant or move into a new local authority and become lost to the system because they are unregistered and cannot be traced. Although many children are considered to be missing from the school system, local authorities hold no definitive figures of exactly how many children of school age reside in its catchment area. In a survey of students who are permanently excluded it was found that a quarter had simply vanished from the system that is legally obliged to educate them (Bourne, 1994). This should be of concern not just to families and practitioners but to society at large because these are the children who grow up to be adults with few options, often living on the margins of society.

The DfES (2003) recognises that transition from primary to secondary school age 11 can put children at risk. Changes to children occur both externally in terms of the school environment and internally as they cope with adolescence.

The Social Exclusion Unit

The Social Exclusion Unit (SEU) was set up in December 1997 in an attempt to reduce social exclusion. It is made up of civil servants and secondees from local authorities, housing, the police, the voluntary sector, social services, faith communities and the probation service. Parliamentary ministers oversee the unit and it works closely with Whitehall and government departmental officials.

The approach of the Social Exclusion Unit includes engaging in wide-ranging consultation and developing partnerships at local level to promote bottom-up initiatives such as Local Strategic Partnerships. The SEU identified what it considers to be five key areas of concern

- truancy and school exclusion (May 1998)
- sleeping rough (1998)
- teenage pregnancy (1999)
- bridging the gap – New opportunities for 16-19 years olds not in education, employment or training (1999)
- neighbourhood renewal (1998/2000/2001)

Within nine months the SEU published a report in which it pointed to the fact that for a minority of young people poverty, family conflict, poor educational opportunities and poor services create a life of under-achievement and social exclusion (Adams, 2002). It proposed a national strategy for neighbourhood renewal, suggesting that eighteen intersecting Policy Action Teams be established. These had two objectives:

- to bridge the gap between the most deprived neighbourhoods and the rest of England

- to achieve lower long-term worklessness, less crime, better health and better educational qualifications

The Policy Action Teams worked in deprived areas to ensure that their recommendations were evidence based and reality tested. Policy Action Team 12 produced a report which identified the aspects of disproportionate disadvantage for people from ethnic minority communities (SEU, 1998b) which intersected all forms of social exclusion. These were:

- poor housing
- unemployment
- ill health
- racial harassment and racist crime
- under-achievement and exclusion from school

Social exclusion has been a key concern on the government's agenda. They have made education a priority and the European Social Fund released money for the creation of social inclusion initiatives nationally to focus on including the excluded. Education is perceived as central to promoting social inclusion. A number of social inclusion initiatives operate throughout the UK to provide education other than at school (EOTAS).

EOTAS projects are funded by monies which usually go to schools via two main funding streams:

- central government gives general school capitation monies to schools via Local authorities (LEAs)
- targeted funding streams for specific initiatives such as the Ethnic Minority Achievement Grant and Excellence in Cities designed to tackle underachievement

These monies follow specific groups of pupils. At the start, teachers targeted certain numbers of pupils. Now there are local strategic partnerships who oversee the allocation of these funds. There were instances of representatives from organisations jostling for position in a constructed hierarchy of deprivation, even though central government had prioritised target populations for raising the educational achievement of Caribbean African boys or white working-class boys. In effect, it appeared that certain organisations benefited from schools and local authority initiatives and colluded to marginalise certain communities, albeit sometimes inadvertently. This practice requires discussion in what could be a difficult conversation.

Funding special provision in education

In 1966, the Home Office set aside funding to support the teaching of children of immigrants. This Section 11 money was used to support the English language learning needs of children for whom English was an additional language (EAL). This was supplanted by the Ethnic Minority Achievement Grant (EMAG) which funds the Ethnic Minority Achievement teams in local authorities. There is a developed teaching practice within EMA teams but it remains predominantly EAL-focused. It took some years before some of the funds were used to support what was called African Caribbean achievement, thus extending EMA's remit and the EMA teams. There have been some attempts to close gaps in attainment between different pupil groups.

The local authority has a duty to educate all pupils, so when a student is excluded from school monies are reallocated to the new relevant education provider. Since March 2004 the excluding school loses its funding for a pupil once an independent appeal panel decides not to direct that pupil's reinstatement. If there is no appeal, on the day after the last date which an appeal may be made, or on the day (if earlier) that the relevant person notifies the local authority that they do not intend to appeal, the excluding school loses its funding for that pupil. Previously the excluding school would lose funding on the day the school's governing body decided that the pupil should not be reinstated. This new date aims to provide schools with continuing funding so that they can arrange education for permanently excluded pupils while they remain on the roll of the excluding school. But new arrangements are not always made and excluded students are sometimes forgotten or ignored.

> She was excluded and so we appealed. In the end we sent her to school in Jamaica with her grandparents. No-one in the education department ever got back to us. (Parent of excluded child)

Parents are left to struggle to obtain school work for their child. This can be a disheartening and devastating exercise.

> I was told he would be sent school work, he has been out of school for 18 months with only half day a week at the cabin. (Parent of excluded child)

Monies are allocated to the new school from the date the pupil enters it. The local authority keeps the difference between these two amounts to contribute towards the time when the pupil is educated out of school.

If no school place is found for them, the local authority keeps the entire amount deducted for education out of school. These transfers of money must be completed within three months of the relevant exclusion date. It is these monies that are used to pay for EOTAS as provided by community-based projects and other initiatives.

My research indicates that some students are never placed in new schools or other educational provision, never receive adequate home tuition – in some cases none at all – and the monies stay in the education department. The motivation for keeping a child in school seems less driven by the goal of education than by budget considerations.

Social inclusion in practice

Radical change is possible. For example, at a conference sponsored by the National Council of School Leaders the attempt to form genuine and authentic partnerships between schools and communities generated uncomfortable but important conversations about the human impact of exclusion and the part played by educators in the under-achievement statistics. School-based teachers, educators and community service providers left with a new shared understanding, vowing to make changes in their establishments.

EOTAS providers are increasingly the new schooling for excluded pupils. These funded projects have stakeholder conditions attached to the funding they receive, for example project evaluations must be carried out to satisfy funders. So projects carry out evaluations which may be based largely on anecdotal evidence. To date there is little rigorous published research that systematically examines social inclusion practice. The sparse local, sub-regional, regional, national and European research on social exclusion confirms that greater resources are needed to respond to this deeply entrenched problem and to ensure that projects for excluded children are regularly and carefully evaluated.

I examined and evaluated several community-based projects, including a project funded from a Social Regeneration Budget (SRB). This sat within an education business partnership (EBP) which was the lead body in an inner city local authority responsible for promoting, co-ordinating and delivering education-business activities aimed at raising the educational attainment of 15 to 19 year olds. The project existed to facilitate inclusion and raise educational attainment amongst the students who were excluded or at risk of exclusion and to re-integrate excluded children into mainstream school.

Another project operated in a relatively leafy urban borough that has a broad geographical stretch of residents with wide ranging needs. Some parts of the borough house middle-class residents but the initiative where some of this research was carried out served an area which was considered to be deprived and in need of regeneration. The area suffered high unemployment and disaffection. Much of it was run down and under threat from property developers.

Both projects expressed concern about the ways in which they were funded and how precarious the funding process was for EOTAS providers.

The projects shared specific objectives:

- to raise the educational achievement of its target population
- to increase social participation of its target population
- to raise the quality and effectiveness of education and training

To move beyond the problem of exclusion to identify solutions and raise achievement among marginalised young people, I examined the philosophy that underpins UK mainstream school education, and the organisational structure and operation of several UK and US community-focused initiatives.

I looked at a community-based initiative which aimed to reconnect disaffected African and Caribbean African young people born and living in the UK with their heritage, by creating opportunities for them to travel to the heritage country and engage with its indigenous people. The rationale was that they would have a real experience rather than an abstract view culled from books or the media.

Another community-based initiative was a rites of passage programme. Life cycle development is a traditional guided process to assist young people to grasp cultural norms. The term rites of passage was not used to describe a practice which was intrinsic to the community until the phrase first appeared in the publication *oLes rites de passageo* (1906).

Through rites of passage processes, young men and women are instructed by young adults and elders in the community and culturally sensitive teachers (*Mwalimu*), who take them through life-related learning relating to their positive intellectual, spiritual, social, emotional and physical development in social contexts. This, according to Karenga (1990), is in keeping with the ancient Kemetic practices to nurture five dimensions of African character: divinity, perfectibility, free will, the need to be morally and socially responsible and teachability (1990).

Inclusion practitioners

Inclusion practitioners can be teachers, tutors, youth workers, group and family workers. To understand socially inclusive practice it is important to look at the principles that guide their practice.

DfES guidelines suggest that exclusion should only be used when all other alternatives have been exhausted. However, there is no published empirical research in the UK that supports this guidance. Teachers are required to be inclusive without being given a standardised approach for doing so. So practitioners working in education have the burden of individually interpreting policy to inform their practice while also dealing with the demands of the national curriculum, SATs and class sizes. With the constantly increasing demands on their time and energy, teachers can be tempted to exclude any child they perceive to be challenging.

Interventions are not neat parcels of involvement, not a matter of two hours of counselling or four hours of mentoring. Humans are complex beings who continually evolve. Accordingly, a model is required that can be disseminated and understood by all the practitioners, parents and students involved in the world of teachers working with children.

If the government push is for inclusion, are there rules of principle and behaviour which distinguish socially inclusive practice from other practice? This work seeks to bring together commonalities of the inclusion practitioner and other people involved through the eyes of those disproportionately affected and determine rules and principles of behaviour by identifying:

- the profile of the inclusive practitioner
- what inclusive practitioners do
- how a socially inclusive initiative functions
- a model of inclusive practice

4

Difficult conversations

They're just sort of ... they ... they are workers but it's not like they ... they're they're friendly ... they're nothing like teachers or anything ... They're sort of down to earth sort of ... proper really down to earth.
(Young Person)

This chapter argues for the need for dialogue, however uncomfortable this might be. There is also a need for new thinking to arrest the widening gulf between inclusion as a concept and what it's like in practice. It does not seek to attribute blame *per se* but to encourage accountability. Adults cannot continue to absolve themselves of responsibility by pathologising children and making them accountable for their plight. It cannot be right to place the blame for exclusion entirely on the excluded child. Difficult conversations, which evaluate all contributing factors, historical and recent, are urgently needed to overturn the 'silent catastrophe' that affects us all.

Difficult conversations about racism

Concepts of race have a history rooted in ideologies of supremacy. They are affected by a changing picture of forced or voluntary migration of people. Race is an extremely problematic term, often used loosely along with the term racist. Fear of being the target of racism or being labelled a racist can inhibit the conversations society needs so much.

When the profile of excluded young people is analysed racism features as a critical trigger for marginalising behaviours. Racism is not the only subject of the difficult conversation but it is a significant part of it. Tackling issues of racism will engage with the issues of marginalisation and oppression. Difficult conversations about racial discrimination in schools is critical but teachers may resist them. Practitioners who fail to recognise the part they play in the practice of exclusion perpetuate exclusion. They prevent an examination of any indicators of children becoming at risk of exclusion.

> *I find it difficult to engage with diverse populations and know that I can't tell the parents or my line manager.* (Teacher)

Some teachers perceive young African men as threatening (Sewell, 1997). African children form 81 per cent of exclusions and yet are only two per cent of the population (*The Observer,* 8 January 1995). This is a group who are disproportionately excluded.

In interviews with Tony Sewell (1997), British African boys named the ten factors that make them most vulnerable to exclusion. They are listed in order of importance:

- teachers who are afraid of children and cannot control their classes
- teachers and head teachers who are not consistent
- boring lessons
- teachers who pick on young people because of their hairstyle
- intelligent children being called boffins and getting beaten up
- teachers not explaining their lessons clearly
- teachers not showing African kids respect
- no heating in classrooms
- no African history
- ancillary staff being racist

Sewell's research gave a voice to the most disproportionately excluded group. Clearly, they can see the factors which make them vulnerable.

Take Rachel, a white teacher in a high school as an example. When confronted with African students and parents in large numbers she acknowledges that she feels uncomfortable: 'When the boys are in groups in the corridors it is very intimidating'. She admits that she has to work hard to prevent her behaviour being affected by her fear.

Most of my research participants were African parents and they spoke of their difficulty communicating with certain teachers, especially white women who become tearful and defensive, so compromising the parent. When teachers refuse to explore the possibility that their attitudes and behaviour can lead to unnecessary exclusions because of their own discomfort or careers, it is their pupils who lose out.

The refusal of a practitioner to engage in the debate about racism and its effects in school perpetuates the practice of blaming children for their exclusion. Their refusal may be overt or it may be disguised as indignation at any implication that racism might be a factor. Ryan (1976) describes people who are careful to disassociate themselves from vulgar overt racism as 'victim blamers'.

Majors (2001) argues for a paradigm shift away from the emphasis on cognitive approaches towards a focus on relationships. He suggests that excluding behaviour will dwindle if teachers develop emotional literacy and the willingness to have these difficult conversations. The fear of being seen as racist was frequently raised by teachers. Teachers' denial, oppression, inability or refusal to consider the possibility of racism has affected thousands of children who were excluded or threatened with exclusion.

School exclusions have lasting effects. They affect the family in a way unresearched until now. The parent/school relationship does not occur in a vacuum; it is influenced by social and economic factors. The parent/school relationship is paramount in determining the success of the child (Wright, 1992).

Parents of excluded children can become fearful and stressed. Schools are encouraged to do what they can to explain their aims and policies to parents and to associate parents with their work (HMI, 1985). However, this can be difficult if there is no established positive working relationship with parents, if parents are mistrustful or if they are unaware of their parental entitlement and power (Gold, 2002).

When a pupil is excluded, a parent or carer may be the first adult who speaks to them about the factors that led to the exclusion. This talking is a therapeutic approach used by practitioners in the helping professions. Psychoanalysis – 'the talking cure' – suggests that language can relieve mental suffering. Talking therapies and faith work have aided recovery and contributed to maintaining the good health and well being of excluded pupils and their families. This may, however, only be available from poorly funded community agencies that offer advocacy support and counselling.

I needed someone to talk to, I thought I was going to go out of my mind or [would] hurt somebody (Parent)

Although the exclusion of their child is distressing for parents, there is often nowhere for the parents to go to get such talking therapy. They may internalise the trauma of watching their child being marginalised and believe that he brings them shame and failure. But exclusion means the school has failed the child and not the other way round.

Stress relief is important for family health and well being (Yuen, 1999). Without an outlet for stress, it is likely that most families who experience social exclusion suffer the persistent consequences without the luxury of a therapeutic service to support their reintegration or to examine alternative work or educational options. They may not have the resources and energy to become empowered enough to move beyond the initial trauma.

Philosophies of inclusion

The linked histories of migrant populations who suffered exclusion casts light on today's perpetrators of excluding practices and how the complexity of race, gender, class, culture and ability contribute to marginalisation.

Michel Foucault identifies how individuals construct truth based on their perceived realities and points out that assumptions are often carried unconsciously and never examined (Foucault, 1979; Hall, 1992). Inclusion and exclusion are defined by the constructs of those in power. They shape the behaviour of teachers and are the foundation for existing legislation, guidance and practice.

If we follow Carter Godwin Woodson (1996), history is not just a matter of gathering of facts, but must take account of the social conditions of the period. It is important to explore the social conditions and histories preceding the current discourse of inclusive education.

The current discourse of inclusion is not the product of one government but a discourse developed over the centuries, just as contemporary philosophical thought emerges from earlier philosophies.

French, Spanish, Dutch and Portuguese history is important in the histories of some of the UK marginalised populations and respected European philosophers have made contributions that influenced the treatment of these populations and contemporary discourse about them.

The philosophical perspectives I inherited were those of European philosophers such as Montesquieu, Hume, Heidegger and Kant. The doctrine of first world rich European greatness (white supremacy) and its correlative hypothesis of third world poverty-stricken Africa (black inferiority) offered by celebrated thinkers of France, Britain and Prussia in the seventeenth century had implications for my experience in higher education. It is paradoxical that Africans are seen as the world's poorest but come from the world's richest continent, not just because of its minerals but also because of earlier civilisations and the contribution to the world as we know it today.

Are there certain distinguishing differences which are used to categorise who will be included and who will not? If so, what are they? This differentiating is an essential step in the pejorative stereotyping of marginalised groups. History shows that in Europe difference has had an extremely detrimental impact on certain populations for example in the practice of eugenics. In ancient Greece difference was seen as representing savageness and in the case of some peoples the difference resulted in notions of sub humanity (Ryan, 1976) which was then used to justify the unequal treatment of fellow humans.

In 2007, the UK commemorated the 200th anniversary of the abolition of the Transatlantic slave trade Act. At the time of writing the UK government refused to apologise for the role Britain played in the abhorrent treatment of people from Africa prior to the abolition of the so called Transatlantic slave trade, merely issuing a statement of regret. Some of the diasporan African community are of the opinion that an apology will not be forthcoming because at the time of the African MA'AFA, Africans were considered less than human, so the claim is that there was no crime against humanity and therefore nothing to apologise for.

> As a compromise it was agreed that text stating it [the British Government] acknowledges and profoundly regrets the massive human sufferings and the tragic plight of millions of men, women and children as a result of slavery, slave trade, transatlantic slave trade, apartheid, colonial-

ism and genocide would be issued. It is expected that a statement of regret will be considered for March 25, 2007. Whitehall is said to believe that while a statement of regret falls short of a formal apology, it would nevertheless be seen as one to mark the anniversary of the date that the Abolition Act was passed by Parliament. (www.ligali.org)

Among the diasporan African community there is a strong belief that the UK Government believes an apology would imply admitting to crimes against humanity and provide grounds for reparation. This is an economic discussion that those in positions of power are not prepared to enter into because it would be too difficult and uncomfortable.

Conversations about terminology

One difficult conversation might examine the use of language to describe the events which affected great numbers of innocent people. The conversation might reveal that Christopher Columbus invaded a population who knew very well where they were and so did not need to be discovered and dispossessed. These people lived with and were sustained by the land they inhabited. History lessons might make it clear how sugar cane, rum and cotton provided by the forced labour of captured people supplied the resources that made Britain great. The difficult conversation would need to be sensitive to the distress this is likely to cause to direct descendants of this exploitation – the so-called slave 'trade' which was in fact human trafficking.

Whilst the act of enslavement is outlawed, what remains is the legacy of enslavement; the inherited consequences, learned behaviour toward one group by another and the unearned privileges of one group at the cost of the other (Gordon, 2007). One legacy of enslavement is the extent to which some children are systematically marginalised, discriminated against and traumatised by a school system that once viewed them as educationally sub-normal and now views them as disruptive and anti-social.

In 1965 certain local authorities such as Ealing and Haringey recommended a policy of pupil dispersal. This resulted in the daily bussing of approximately 3,000 Asian immigrant pupils to schools where they would make up less than 20 per cent of any class (Dhondy, 1985). Systems of banding streamed young Caribbean African students into classes which were designed for the educationally sub-normal, describing them as ESN and placing them in schools which in effect put paid to their education (Coard, 1971). This led to an over-representation of Caribbean African young people in sink schools, lower sets and the ranks of the under-achievers (Gillborn, 2001).

The need for training of teachers was highlighted in my interviews with parents, students and teachers themselves. Several teachers admitted that they felt ill-equipped to work with inner city children with their 'gansta rap and jeans round their thighs'.

Difficult conversations about worldviews

Only recently has a balanced world history of marginalised communities begun to be taught in school. Schools used to teach African history by beginning with the so called transatlantic slave trade. This did nothing for the self-esteem of children of African heritage and promoted negative associations with Africa. Much of this teaching was part of post-colonial teaching practice that convinced people from the Caribbean that Africa was poor, diseased and malnourished. Diop (1978) argues that the history of humankind lacks the correct African history. He maintains that the object of historical study is to arrive at a reasonable interpretation of the facts and that history is more than political and military records of peoples and nations.

Algerian philosopher Louis Pierre Althusser asserted that it was possible to study politics, law and philosophy as activities which are independent of economic production. He argued that recognition of economics contributed not to the development of people but to the development of wealth. Althusser's most controversial idea was that Marxism was not a moral philosophy concerned with the alienation of humankind under capitalism and its possible redemption under socialism but that it was a science and was anti-human.

Franz Fanon (1967) argues that economics is the base for a neo-colonialism, a new age kind of colonialism. If economics is seen as nothing to do with the development and wellbeing of people but is simply about budgets and wealth generation, regardless of human cost, this is bound to affect those once considered to be only three fifths human and who are still not considered deserving of a remembrance day or an apology for the massacre of millions of their ancestors in crimes and wars. These conversations are difficult but necessary to bring about new understanding and the healing of a great hurt.

My reading made me see a link between school exclusion experienced by Caribbean African young people in UK schools and the historical practice of excluding African people and thus placing them at a social, psychological and economic disadvantage. Contrast this with a view of inclusive practice, perspectives, histories and peoples that is presented from the perspective of pupils affected by school exclusion. I propose a new perspective underpinned by a philosophical and economical link between the past and the present, since inclusion is closely linked to issues of economics and income generation.

Notions of superiority and inferiority have links to notions of inclusion and exclusion where mainstream is seen as better than an alternative education provision. This hegemonic approach excludes other world-views and practices, preventing them from taking their place alongside mainstream without hierarchy or hegemony. Viewing phenomena from an African-centred perspective and locating myself as central rather than peripheral, secured a better vantage point from which to consider the facts and permitted an alternative perspective to the usual one of being researched, measured and interpreted using European-centred frames of reference.

Alternative philosophies can be understood in the same way as alter-native research methods such as the phenomenological, ethno methodological. The concepts can be grasped if the fundamental prin-ciples are understood. Afri-centrism basis its philosophy on cultural symbolisms which embrace a particular moral and spiritual code and allows for the grasping of theoretical and philosophical bases which in-corporate matters spiritual as central. It legitimises intuition, dream interpretation and meditation – all metaphysical components which impact on African ways of being.

Western society dictates the conveying of knowledge and compliant be-haviour in a systematic endeavour to create order. However it is ques-tionable how an approach which is based on philosophies which do not include alternative ways of being and knowing (Foucault, 1979) can be properly inclusive.

Marginalised communities are seldom consulted in meaningful way for their perspective on the lived causes and consequences of their ex-clusion. The prevailing approach is informed by people outside of the experience with a narrowly Eurocentric view of the world. These people cannot inhabit the physical and philosophical spaces of certain marginalised communities.

An alternative worldview sees nature as a friend to be in tune with and acknowledge. Spirituality facilitates this tuning (Heidegger, 1955) or harmonising with nature, the cosmos, universe and The God Force (Nantambu, 1996).

> This alternative ideology and belief system exhibit characteristically African conceptions of the relationship between art and life, the sacred and the secular, the spiritual and the material and traces of these African formulations remain, albeit in displaced and mediated forms, even in the folk philosophies, religion and vernacular arts of black Britain. (Gilroy, 2006)

An African-centred worldview value system is characterised by spirituality, persistence, caring, communalism and co-operativism based in principles of *MA'AT* and the *NGUZO SABA,* Kiswahili words for spiritual systems and principles of governance. These principles of truth, justice, righteousness, reciprocity, balance, harmony and order are an integral part of an African-centred worldview

> Afrocentricity is an uncovering of one's true self, it is the pinpointing of one's centre and it is the clarity and focus through which black people must see the world... (Gilroy, 2002)

MA'AT

MA'AT is a spiritual knowledge system and the concept of *MA'AT* brings a language of moral philosophy and ethical theory building that assists in the reconnection to the matrix of cultural backgrounds.

Cultural strengthening is important in assisting Diasporan communities to affirm their spiritual, emotional and intellectual health. This strengthening of marginalised communities supports the claims to intellectual spaces and the articulation of experiences by a population which has been historically silenced in the discourse of European male intellectual hegemony. Human relationships that foreground empathy, social justice, truth and reciprocity are the process through which *MA'AT* is made real so that it is part of daily living and not an abstract theory.

MA'AT unifies space and time, harmonising young and old, male and female, past and present, the living, the departed and those yet to be born. The forging of unity rather than separateness reduces distance and disconnection. It is healing. This healing in and of a marginalised population is transformational and can restore and create visions, futures and raise the educational achievement of a population excluded from the discourse of inclusion. In a *MA'AT*ian system individuals are valued and self-actualisation is accelerated in morally grounded relationships that recognise that people are members of communities and that to exclude is harmful not only to the person but to the family, the community and ultimately to society. *MA'AT* promotes inclusion and the notion that the collective and the individual are closely interlinked and that to harm one is to harm both similar to the philosophy of Martin Luther King which was that injustice anywhere is a threat to injustice everywhere.

African-centred approaches to education

African-centred orientations to education identify marginalisation, exclusion and rejection as oppressive and as a source of current problems of under-achievement and social disorder. To date education has not been afforded the discourse about the consequence of spiritual alienation in explaining and resolving exclusion problems. Spiritual alienation frustrates, depresses and impedes the creation of visions and possibilities in people so that dreams are often deferred or lost.

Education is largely uninformed about the interpretations and understandings of socio-cultural perspectives that emerge from African communities. In response Diasporan communities have created cultural, academic and other spaces where the undiscussed is voiced and a new understanding can be reached without the restriction of having to pacify other groups. One such organisation is the Colloquium of African-descended academics and practitioners, based on an idea by academic Dr Mekada Graham and is part of the intellectual exodus by those who cannot realise academic aspirations in a hostile Euro-centric climate. The Colloquium exists to raise the confidence of African-centred academics and to facilitate a new body of knowledge. The aims of the Colloquium are to:

- encourage African-descended academics and practitioners to write and publish from within their own lived experiences

66

- encourage those who write from within the African experience to do so critically and from an African-centred not a Euro-centric standpoint

- forge a relationship with academics and practitioners that supports the development of new themes and ideas for a home-grown African-centred philosophy and perspective

At their 2006 conference, members of the Black Research Colloquium in the UK attested to experiencing isolation and marginalisation in schools and to feeling invisible in higher education. This created an intellectual space for discourse from an African-centred perspective.

The colloquium is creating the vehicle for the intellectual, physical, social and spiritual well-being of individuals and communities from the Diaspora. Through the affirmation of the connections between spirituality, collective consciousness, intellectual and socio-political agency, spiritual knowing and human emotions become legitimate and intelligible knowledge.

> The Colloquium is a response to the section of the academic population who believe that writing from an African-centred perspective will lead to academic suicide.

> ...to inform those who have been misinformed by interpretations provided through lenses that question and make value judgements about others, not from their perspectives but from an experience that bears little resemblance to those under the microscope. (The Colloquium of African-Descended Academics and Practitioners, 2007)

Spiritual knowing entails the individual sharing experiences of the universal meaning of human existence through being in community and being in relationship to other people (Miller, 1999 cited in Dei, 1999). In this context spirituality supplies the context and meaning for communities.

> African-centred approaches consider these aspects of self as central to harmony and well being and are nurtured via conceptions of personhood through and within connections with family, social networks and communities. (Graham, 2001)

One of the ways in which an African-centred worldview differs from a western perspective can be found in the distinguishing feature of western philosophical practice. Western philosophers argue for their thesis, clarifying meaning and answering objections, known or anticipated. In alternative traditions philosophies do not base their discourse on defence and argument.

> It is important to point out that the claim that Africans have no theoretical or scientific thought is not only erroneous but misleading. (Wiredu, 1987)

In some cultures the transmitter of folk conceptions (philosophy) merely says: This is what our Ancestors said: the tradition is oral (Wiredu, 1987). Too often practitioners are so steeped in their practice that they simply relay it but do not write it down or defend it. The Colloquium provides an intellectual space for the presentation of African-centred systematic and rigorous research.

Alternative ways of knowing place Spirit as primary and African-centred methodology redefines reality to incorporate the spiritual (Ani, 1994). It includes the concept of an extended-self which reflects balance in value and understanding for both rational empirical and spiritual methods of knowing. It also acknowledges the idea of a genetic memory.

> *I remember my Ancestors all the time even though I did not meet them. The things they went through help me to go through being undermined by my colleagues. I know I might not be making sense right now but I know what I mean and how I feel.* (African University Lecturer)

There have been questions about whether we can say without doubt that we live in entirely separated, divided and distinguished worlds (Hollis, 1997). Global warming is an example of the way in which there is no separation of consequence. What we can agree is that we have differing worldviews. This links us back to the need for practices that include alternative knowledge because increasing exclusion rates will have a strong impact on social stability and economic competitiveness.

In cultures where spiritual practice and knowledge is uppermost and people consider that the invisible is more real than the visible, there is greater hope and stronger faith (Akbar, 2002). This hope and faith is relevant to this research investigation. As a response to what Diane Abbott has called the 'silent catastrophe' of African boys being failed by the UK education system, Caribbean African communities set up supplementary schools. Many are housed in organisations based on faith and hope but they are not necessarily overtly religious (Hylton, 1999). Rather culture and spirituality are seen not as an add-on but as an intrinsic part of life.

To be African-centred places the African and African worldviews at the centre not at the margin: African matters are not peripheral, especially when examining events that impact differently on people of African descent. African-centrism recognises that cause and effect operate at all times. This is a more complex construct than Karma, the idea that there is a consequence for every action: all dynamics operate simultaneously all the time and the consequence is enduring. In an African-centred worldview the earthly and the spiritual are constant and accepted without question whereas in the European worldview philosophical questions are asked such as whether or not a tree makes a noise when it falls and no one is around to hear it. To an African-centred philosopher, this question is irrelevant.

Philosophy, then, contributes to how individuals and society view and interpret the world and what is considered relevant or important. Schools are shaped by the philosophers past and present whether politicians or researchers. The significance of things seen or unseen and how this influences agendas depends upon the perspective and philosophy of the person, organisation or system viewing the phenomenon. It is essential to afford African philosophy a central position when considering matters that affect everyone but it is critical when trying to understand the perspective and lived experience of African people. In matters which affect people who originate from Africa it is a deliberate act of exclusion to marginalise, subjugate or omit African knowledge and experience. In light of the differences between African-centred and European-centred world-views there will be difficult conversations about teachers' professional development. There may be a declared agenda to create a society that includes everyone. But it is not clear how this will be implemented without specialist training being provided for all professionals involved in the delivery of education for all.

5

Systems of schooling in
England and Wales

M uch of Labour's discourse on rights and responsibilities stems
from the writings and recommendations of the Commission
on Social Justice. This was set up by the late leader of the
Labour Party, John Smith to try and mitigate the exclusion of growing
numbers of young people from certain social groups and people with
disabilities. One of the main recommendations of the Commission's
Report (1994) was that paid work was the key to social inclusion and
remained the best route out of poverty:

> employment is inseparable from individual opportunity ... paid work re-
> mains the best pathway out of poverty, as well as the only way in which
> most people can hope to achieve a decent standard of living. ... Without
> jobs there can be no justice. (CSJ, 1994: 151).

Politics and policy
In 1976 Prime Minister James Callaghan introduced the needs of the
economy into the great debate of social inclusion. He stated that there
is no virtue in producing socially well-adjusted members of society who
are then unemployed because they do not have the skills the country
needs.

Since then there has been a stream of publications on the subject.
Governments have produced circulars designed to offer schools
guidance about providing schooling for young people. The Department
for Education published Circulars 8/94 and 9/94, giving the message

that expert teaching and skilled behaviour lessened disaffection and disruption (Daniels and Sellman, 2003). But any pupils who were disruptive were considered to have a problem – it was never seen as the fault of the practitioners. Exclusion was the fault of the child, who bore the full burden of cause and consequence. Even now, as my research found, teachers close ranks and collude with school governors to support the headteacher's decision, right or wrong to exclude a child.

> *I didn't agree with the exclusion but the head had made up her mind and it is her school.* (Head of Year)

The tendency remains to adapt the child to the school and reject any pupil who does not readily fit into predetermined notions of conformity. For instance the Education Act 1993, whilst giving parents the choice of educating their children in mainstream school, included allowances for exceptions and so released schools from the legal obligation to adapt to meet the needs of a pupil, even a child with a statement of special education needs (SEN).

New Labour's landslide victories in 1997 and 2001 allowed them to re-formulate policies and win the support of many middle-class voters who were dissatisfied with Tory politics. The Secretary of State for Education and Employment directed LEAs to work towards getting the learning needs of pupils who had special needs met in mainstream school provision. According to the Green Paper on special education:

> While recognising the paramount importance of meeting the needs of individual children and the necessity of specialist provision for some, we shall promote the inclusion of children with SEN within mainstream schooling wherever possible. (DfEE, 1997:5)

This thinking also informs the Code of Practice of 2001 (DfES).

The Connexions Strategy as set out in DfES Guidance (0070/2000) is aimed to bring together a range of services for young people aged 13 to 19 (Gold, 2002). This is a more flexible approach to educating young people. The need for flexibility is reflected in the DfEE's caveats to full inclusion:

> For some children, a mainstream placement may not be right, or not right just yet. We therefore confirm that specialist provision – often, but not always, in special schools – will continue to play a vital role (DfEE 1998:23)

Education as a right

The International Convention on the Rights of the Child recognises every child's right to education. In England and Wales legislation merely indicates that children must be in full time education suited to their ability and aptitude (Gold, 2002). Provision for compulsory education for 5-16 year olds is divided into: primary and secondary and most secondary schools are comprehensive.

Local authorities have a responsibility to provide suitable full time education for students excluded for a fixed period of over fifteen days and all permanently excluded pupils. In addition they are expected to re-integrate pupils, where practical, as quickly as possible into a suitable mainstream school. Students who are excluded from school premises are not considered excluded from education and have Key Stage related education entitlement. Weekly education entitlement for excluded pupils is identified as 21 hours for pupils aged 5 to 7 (KS1), $23^1/_2$ hours for pupils aged 7 to 11 (KS2) and 24 hours for pupils aged 11 to 14 (KS3) and 14 to 16 (KS4) (DfES guidance in Circular 7/90).

The Pupil Referral Units (PRUs) who provide this education are registered with the DfES and administered by the local LEA, so they follow guidance issued by the DfES. Students on the register of a PRU were originally entitled to three sessions or classes but this has risen to ten sessions, amounting to 20 hours provision per week – although many students receive less.

The statistics produced in Social Exclusion Unit Policy Action Team 12 research suggests that the vulnerable groups of children identified are those who are more likely to be excluded. Reimer (1971) suggests that children who never go to school are the most deprived in the long term, both economically and politically.

Accountability

The timetable of an excluded student may differ from their previous mainstream school curriculum timetable and they may attend one or a number of education sites. Efforts are expected to be made to reintegrate students, so that alternative provision does not become a barrier to re-inclusion. The government emphasis on reintegration suggests that school is the best learning environment because it provides access to the full National Curriculum, support, activities and social interaction. PRUs are an expensive provision, so it makes educational and economic sense to retain students in schools.

Panels are expected to meet regularly to discuss the education provision for excluded pupils and the meeting might include involvement from education welfare officers, social services representatives – especially if the child is looked after by the authority or on the child protection register – educational psychologists, staff from the PRU or other providers of education outside school (eg further education institutions and social inclusion initiatives), local authority admissions personnel, SEN policy staff and other professionals with inclusion responsibility, school staff (eg head teachers, pastoral support staff), community representatives and representatives of other interest groups.

Since they are responsible for providing education, local authorities should quality assure the provision offered and be monitoring attendance and pupil outcomes. I found that this does not always happen, because of staff shortages, lack of qualified evaluators and budget constraints. Since 1993, the Office for Standards in Education (Ofsted) carries out all inspections of schools and PRUs.

Government research indicates a link between lack of education and crime. To facilitate social inclusion they work to address the problem through government neighbourhood renewal strategies such as the New Deal for Communities (NDC) programme. However, they recognise that lasting change is dependent on a variety of approaches and on sustained capacity building programmes that work in partnerships. In the 2000 comprehensive spending review of the national strategy for neighbourhood renewal the treasury has assigned budgets for raising the achievement of under-achieving children in mainstream school provision in partnership collaborations.

Securing a mainstream placement is not synonymous with inclusion, as many students are in mainstream placements but have the National Curriculum dis-applied by a statement of special educational needs or in when the head teacher considers that the National Curriculum is inappropriate (Gold, 2002). Pupils may even be dual registered – on the register of a mainstream provision but attending offsite education provision. Other children may be attending mainstream school but excluded from classes. In these instances the school receives the budgetary allocation attached to the student without having the responsibility of teaching them (Bourne, 1994).

74

Schooling

This section looks at the purpose, organisation and categorisation of schools in an attempt to illustrate the way in which issues of exclusion and excluding behaviours have existed and become legitimised.

As Haki R. Madhubuti observed:

> There is a profound difference between going to school and being educated. (Shujaa, 1994)

Schooling is intended to perpetuate and maintain a society's existing power relations and the institutional structures that support those arrangements (Shujaa, 1994). It provides a systematic mechanism for entry, information delivery, tracking, testing and reward and is influenced by the structural conditions, political and economic requirement of the society in which it is situated. Education, however, is about probing deeply to find a student's essential qualities and knowledge and bring them out (Simon, 2006).

The plight of disaffected young people in Britain is embedded in a practice of delivering education that is intended to shape their academic and educational outcomes. This pedagogy of delivery is based on a long tradition of English schooling and more recent national curriculum key stage targets which provide little or no accommodation for the background, social and learning needs, physical requirements or cultural communities of pupils. The methods and rationale for delivery in mainstream school is founded in a problematic philosophical history which is unfavourable towards children of African and Caribbean African origin and appearance, as we have seen.

However, concern about the consequences of social exclusion has led the government to explore how this can be tackled in education. But it has restricted its view of education as being about nothing but schools, yet my study shows that many young people who have achieved little during their compulsory schooling excel educationally in the years thereafter.

Reimer (1971) identifies four distinct functions which facilitate the development of the knowledge and skills of societal norms:

- custodial care
- social role selection

■ indoctrination
■ education

Schools are instruments of privilege. Dhondy (1985) views schooling as the internal, partly benevolent, colonialisation over fifteen thousand hours of the lives of the young by the school workforce of academic and pastoral teams.

Historically the British education system has always been selective and divisive. Below the public schools for the elite came the grammar schools, created for the offspring of merchants and the middle classes and public and civil servants. The 1944 Education Act introduced schooling as a provision for the majority of children and schools have developed different characteristics over the years. Secondary moderns were local schools for local people to go to after primary school. It was where you went if you failed your 11 plus and did not get into a grammar school.

In the 1960s and 70s schools were reorganised on comprehensive lines and the pass entrance exams was scrapped. Comprehensive schools were based the idea of ensuring equality of opportunity for all young people and of accommodating young people at the other end of the social scale.

The many types of schools include community schools, voluntary, voluntary aided and foundation schools (Gold, 2002). Community Schools are wholly funded by the local authority and staff are employed by the LEA. Voluntary aided schools usually have a religious denomination or independent foundation in the form of a charity. Secondary schools are now giving way to academies. These new academies are exempt from certain expectations to gain an academic qualification. They do not have to deliver the national curriculum, and offer their students GNVQs, competence based vocational qualification.

Schools were never designed for the working class or for Africans. Public schools were not available to the general population and were originally created for the sons and daughters of aristocracy and gentry. The students were children of the elite, leaders and entrepreneurs.

The differing philosophies of the Welsh, Scottish and Irish members of the British Commonwealth influenced the intellectual life of England. The place of education was of more importance than the place of birth, origin or appearance. Scottish, Irish and Welsh scholars were not particularly welcomed in the early English public schools either (Hans, 1966), just as young people from the Caribbean (Dhondy, 1985) and elsewhere find today.

Schools are places of social interaction. So they can be contentious institutional environments, where an individual's worth is measured by achievement (qualifications) and by human qualities, appearance or ability. This can make children fearful of making mistakes. It is hardly conducive to learning. For an increasing number of Caribbean African students mistakes are a luxury. They complain bitterly that they cannot get social justice.

> *Things are not fair in school; the black kids are picked on all the time.*
> (European boy)

Special schools

Special schools emerged in response to growing needs for a special kind of education for young people who might have needs that were thought to be outside the responsibility of state schools. They developed as a new human rights report called for the phased closure of separate special schools, which were seen as a threat of developing inclusive education. A report for the Centre for Studies on Inclusive Education (Rustemier, 2002) declares that segregated schooling violates children's rights. The report recommended that all resources from special schools should be transferred to mainstream settings, which should be restructured to increase their capacity to respond to student diversity in its entirety. The report claimed that the central problem in the development of inclusive education in the UK is the continuing philosophical, financial and legislative support for segregated schooling.

It argued that segregation in separate special schools is internationally recognised as being discriminatory and damaging to individuals and society. As well as violating children's rights to inclusive education, segregated schooling breaches the principles underpinning the 1989 UN Convention on the Rights of the Child. The report acknowledged progress in developing the capacity of mainstream schools in the UK to enable all children and young people to learn together but stressed that special schools remained a fundamental obstacle to inclusion.

Adoption of the term inclusion into common education language could signify a genuine desire to improve the experience of all learners. Yet in many cases it seems to be a concept which is misunderstood or even deliberately distorted. Contrary to ideas of social justice, it has become widely accepted that there are exceptions to who can be included. Rustemier (2002) maintains that inclusion has come to mean almost everything but the elimination of exclusion.

Ever since the 1700s notions existed of educational sub-normality. The 1921 Education Act states that you need to be very dull or backward to be ESN, and an IQ of 50 or under meant you were an imbecile. The tests determining IQ were linguistically and culturally biased. By the end of world war two special education became a feature of state education.

The pressure for inclusion and equal education for Caribbean African students originally came from Caribbean African activists in the UK, the Civil Rights Movement in America in the 1960s and 1970s and the parents of so-called disaffected pupils (Comer, 1992). In recent years practitioners, academics, politicians and other concerned individuals and parties have called for a more inclusive system of education.

Supplementary schools

The national Supplementary School Movement emerged from a national conference held in January 1972, organised by the Caribbean Education and Community Workers Association (CECWA). The movement for Saturday schools developed out of resistance to bussing and was hugely boosted by Bernard Coard's book (1971).

Activist and interest groups in the 70s, parents and community leaders from the Caribbean African community who felt that their children were not receiving an education which served their best interests, mobilised and created Saturday supplementary schools wherever there were African populations. The intention was that they would complement rather than conflict with what happens in mainstream school.

Pupil referral units (PRUs)

Practices of excluding and refusing entry are long established UK practice, based initially on systems of class and affordability. However, school statistics indicate that current exclusions are linked to more complex matters of vulnerability, deprivation, gender and race.

The government's social inclusion agenda reviewed the provision for young people who display characteristics and behaviours which are not accommodated in mainstream schools. When pupils are excluded from school the local authority still has a statutory duty to provide suitable full or part-time education for them. They may be offered education otherwise than at school (EOTAS) as per Circular 11/94. (DfES, 1994d), referred to as the off site unit, the hut, sin bins (*Sun*, 1975; Daniels, 2003). The alternative school, re-integration service, the social inclusion service and more recently study centres. These provide one of the ways for local authorities to meet their statutory duty. Along with special schools, Primary Behaviour Units and Social Inclusion Centres, PRUs are a hidden place where children are sent. Policies have focused on penalty rather identifying solution focused policies.

PRUs first appeared in 1970 in the ILEA (Dhondy, 1985). The social inclusion agenda takes the view that these placements severely restrict the life chances of young people. Yet there are around 300 study centres nationally. They were established as schools under the Education Act 1996 but are not bound by all the statutory requirements which apply to mainstream schools so do not function in the same way (Gold, 2002).

PRUs are not required to deliver the subjects in the national curriculum or religious education. Although registered as schools for the purpose of receiving DfES, now DCSF, information, PRUs do not have to undertake assessment at the end of the key stages as schools do. The requirements outlined by the DfES include the following:

- Pupil referral units are expected to provide an annual report to parents on pupils progress but there is no statutory requirement to provide reports on the subjects of the national curriculum

- Pupil referral units are expected to deliver a curriculum that satisfies the requirement of being broad and balanced in compliance with the local authority's curriculum policy

- Headteachers and teachers in charge of a PRU must by law have regard to guidance issued by the DfES when making decisions on exclusion and administering the exclusion procedure

The DfES published inclusive recommendations to guide PRUs. Its guidance on students whose parents do not fully understand English recommends that correspondence relating to the exclusion should be translated into their first language and that the PRU or local authority should arrange for an interpreter to be present at any meetings with parents about the exclusion.

Although provided by the government as an education provision otherwise than at school, PRUs are regarded as a less than adequate substitute for full-time schooling (Gold, 2002). Importantly, they are required to publish a policy plan to re-integrate pupils after a relatively short time to mainstream or special schools or to help them to go on to further education or employment (Gold, 2002). No figures are available yet but my research indicates that re-integration does not happen nearly enough.

The catastrophe of exclusion

The extent of school truancy and exclusions causes increasing alarm. According to a Truancy and Social Exclusion Report (Daniels, 2003), some 13,000 young people are permanently excluded every year. Contrary to DfES recommendations, many excluded young people receive as little as three or four hours of tuition each week and many get nothing. Excluded young people are at increased risk of becoming teenage parents, unemployed, homeless or incarcerated. Currently, the government has a target of reducing the level of truancy and the numbers of permanent and fixed-term exclusions by one third.

The Truancy and School Exclusion Report (1998b), indicates that whilst white teenage boys might experience exclusion, there is extensive evidence that other groups suffer staggeringly disproportionate levels of exclusion. Children with special needs are at increased risk of exclusion, as are Caribbean African children who are up to six times more likely to be excluded. And looked after children (children in care) are more than ten times at risk of school exclusion. So for a British born Caribbean African boy with special education needs from a working-class background who is looked after the future is particularly precarious.

Neither the cause nor the effect of exclusion can be understood simply as an educational issue. The consequences reach far beyond educational failure. We have seen that exclusion has an impact on families, communities and society at large. It is an issue that requires joined-up thinking and multi-agency response. The Social Exclusion Unit seeks to bring a cross-departmental focus to exclusion to enable integrated initiatives.

Young people may feel disconnected from mainstream school or displaced in society. The causes and circumstances may vary but the impact is disconnection and displacement, leading to under-achievement and unemployment. Exclusion devastates young people and their families so severely that many are unable to attain qualifications for years after exclusion and their self-esteem may be seriously affected.

Disaffection, low self-esteem, marginalisation and frustration may drive them to a polarised position and result in confusion and ignorance because the norms of the host community are seldom known or understood and may be unachievable or simply rejected.

In addition to the groups identified by the government's Social Exclusion Unit, DfES guidelines suggest that young people at particular risk also include:

- those with special educational needs
- ethnic minority children
- young carers
- those from families under stress
- teenage mothers

Human rights

When Britain joined the European Convention on Human Rights in October 2000, education became a human right. English law became compatible with the International Convention on Human Rights of 1995. Section 4.1. of The Salamanca Statement On Principles, Policy and Practice in Special Needs Education, which arose out of the world conference organised in Spain 1994 by UNESCO states that:

- every child has a fundamental right to education and must be given the opportunity to achieve and maintain an acceptable level of learning

- every child has unique characteristics, interests, abilities and learning needs

■ education systems should be designed and educational programs implemented to take into account the wide diversity of these characteristics and needs

■ those with special educational needs must have access to regular schools which should accommodate them within child centred pedagogy capable of meeting these needs

In short the Salamanca Statement called on the international community to endorse the approach of inclusive schooling and to support the development of special needs education as an integral part of all education programmes.

Prior to the Salamanca Statement a commitment to Education for All by 2000 (EFA, 2000) was made at a high-level conference held in Jomtien, Thailand, organised by UNICEF, UNESCO, the UN Development Programme and the World Bank, with specific reference to disabled children. This commitment was renewed in New York at a one-day Summit on Children (Mittler, 2000).

The Human Rights Act adopted by Britain in 1998 enshrines the right to an education. It informs the right to education and the prohibition of discrimination on the grounds of race, gender and disability. However, it does not entitle parents to insist on a place in a particular school (Gold, 2002). Schools are guided by DfES Guidance 0194/2000, *The Human Rights Act and Your School.*

Factors in marginalisation

Marginalisation began as a class issue based in notions of an underclass. With the arrival of people from British colonies exclusion exploded into much more than a class issue and the systematic approach to young people with visible differences of language, behaviour and appearance seemed to be to marginalise them. Racism is a powerful dimension of the underclass debate. Even in the use of the term 'black' there is implied and explicit marginalisation.

Statistics demonstrate that Asian and continental African young people are excluded less than those with Caribbean African heritage. The media and police talk of black on black violence. No-one else is ever referred to in similar terms.

Issues of class, gender, ability and ethnic origin have powerful effects on educational outcomes (Bhavnani, 2001). Paulo Freire (1921-97) was concerned about the plight of the oppressed and referred to the culture of silence among those who had no voice (Crotty, 1998).

Gender is a variable in exclusion – boys are approximately three times more likely than girls to be excluded. Travellers are the group most disadvantaged in the education system. And emerging bilinguals seldom achieve their potential when all emphasis is on their English and not their first languages.

Language: People who have not learned Greek, Latin or French may not know the origin, root meaning of words and how they are constructed and are more likely to make spelling errors and misuse language. This is not an indicator of low intelligence but a disadvantage – and one that is often overlooked. Those who do not share English as their first language still have a story and their dialect or construction of language does not diminish the importance of that story. The current social inclusion discourse has provided an opportunity for the voiceless pupils, parents and practitioners to be heard but even so, practitioners are so entrenched in traditional practice that they can often be unheard or misunderstood. This is an issue of knowledge of language not dialect. Language becomes standardised due to historical, geographical and social influences, so no dialect is inherently superior or inferior to any other (Stubbs, 1976). Many dialects of English such as spoken in Birmingham, East London, Liverpool, Newcastle as well as Irish, Scottish and Welsh were often regarded as unacceptable and English as spoken in the Southern counties and on the BBC was preferred.

Language is a major instrument of cultural de-personalisation and control. The language of schools can be excluding and oppressive. Until recently, standard English was insisted upon in schools even though it is not the mode of expression among the working-class in England; certain dialects including slang were equated with low ability and intelligence. The ability to speak in conventional ways was incorrectly used as a way to measure ability and intelligence (Stubbs, 1976).

Language and labels can situate people in ways that are dangerously restricting. Unless empowered, a young person can be located in one or more of the following categories just because of how they speak: at risk of disaffection; disaffected; anti social or disruptive.

Class: We cannot focus exclusively on race. We have also to take account of intersecting factors that impinge on exclusion, particularly class. The expectations of the schools for working-class white people were for many years relatively fixed and low expectations were common. In contrast, Caribbean African people viewed education as an important means of social mobility and consequently had high expectations of the school and Caribbean African young people (Dhondy, 1985). The parents put their faith in education:

> Labour for learning before you grow old,
> For learning is better than silver and gold
> Silver and gold will vanish away,
> But a good education will never decay.

The system in England fails many working-class children (Stone, 1981). In the 1950s and 1960s as the British Empire came to an end, the working-class were also oppressed (Freire, 1985). In Victorian times religion was used to endorse the class system, as in the following hymn:

> All things bright and beautiful, all creatures great and small ... rich man in his castle, poor man at his gate, God made them high or lowly and ordered their estate

Author Charles Wesley allegedly claimed that one's position in life was ordained so that '*the working-class are drawers of water and hewers of wood*'.

Looked after children: Children under the care of Social Services are among those most likely to underachieve at school. The research indicates that they are likely to truant and the exclusion rate is high. According to the statistics, one in four looked-after 14 year olds and over do not attend school. As there is a proven link between exclusion, truancy and crime and thus between delinquency and unemployment, children who were looked after are over-represented among the unemployed, the homeless and those involved in crime and abusive situations.

Migrant communities

Voluntary migration took place over generations to fill UK post-war labour shortages. People came from different socio-economic backgrounds (Patterson, 1963). Large numbers of Caribbean people saw themselves as migrant labour arriving in England in response to the call to offer their help to rebuild the UK after the devastating effects of the war (Barrow, 1986). Caribbean Africans arrived intending to spend a few years in the 'mother' country and return to the Caribbean. They faced a hostile reception and had difficulty finding homes. Notices on windows read: 'No Pets, No Irish, No Blacks'.

Nonetheless, they worked for British Rail, London Transport, the National Health Service and other institutions which support the Britain of today. Even Enoch Powell, later to warn that immigration would lead to 'the river flowing with much blood', was actively recruiting nurses from the Caribbean in the 1960s, while Minister for Health. British schools are populated with second and third generation migrants and refugees, transforming the nation's cultural mix for the 21st century.

Physical and non physical impairments

From 2002 it became unlawful to discriminate against people with disabilities and from September 2005 schools were required to make adjustments that involve the provision of auxiliary aids and services if the current premises put disabled people at substantial disadvantage (Gold, 2002).

Looking at the social exclusion of people with disabilities can help us identify more generally with how socially excluding practices can be addressed. Two major models of disability can be readily identified: the medical model, prominent in policy making and the social model. The medical model sees the person as deficient.

Disability used to be defined in terms of a range of discrete clinical conditions and has its origins in medical professionals defining the needs and capacities of people with disabilities. The conditions were all seen as a personal misfortune. This blocked the possibility of recognising disabled persons as a social group who shared the experience of stigma, discrimination, forced dependency and exclusion. The language around disability may have changed but people with impairments have to negotiate and assert themselves to minimise the extent of the disadvantage they face, as is the case for race and gender (Bagihole, 1997: 42).

There are some radical sentiments in New Labour's rhetoric that appear to transcend the individualistic medical model of disability. The Secretary of State for the Department of Social Security in 1998 stated:

> It is too easy to see the problems of people with disabilities as inevitable consequences of their condition. In fact, our society is to blame for the fact that people with disabilities face many difficulties and barriers to leading a fulfilling life, not least the perpetuation of discriminatory attitudes. In all our measures what we are aiming for is a fully integrated and inclusive society in which people with disabilities are given the best opportunities possible. (DSS, 1998)

So there is some movement away from the long-standing medical model of disability to a more social model. Adopting a universal behaviour model exacerbates social difference and creates dilemmas for those classed as severely disabled who are outside the expectations of mainstream society but nonetheless keen to participate in society and receive the benefits and opportunities available to others.

The social model of disability is now largely accepted (Oliver, 1996:64). It focuses on how environmental, structural and attitudinal barriers restrict the opportunity of people to participate in the activities of daily living and in effect disable them. It recognises that the social and physical environment has been designed by people who have given little thought to the needs of others or what it feels like to have to rely on others (Finklestein, 1988). Distinctions can be made between impairment, which is a functional limitation, and disability, which is an opportunity limitation creating social, physical and attitudinal barriers

A study called Everyone Here Spoke Sign Language focused on a small and isolated American community in Martha's Vineyard. There were two distinctive characteristics of this community: the high incidence of profound hereditary deafness; and everyone being bilingual. Members with full hearing often communicated in sign language and did not consider any of the other members disabled. They were simply deaf (Groce, 1995; Oliver, 1996:52).

For generations the citizenship rights of some sectors of society labelled 'disabled' have been systematically infringed. But activists have successfully lobbied for rights. However, I question whether the rhetoric government's about a new political and social settlement based on a third way really offers formerly excluded people new opportunities to be included. This is certainly not the case in educational provision.

Concentrating on populations of young people based on ethnicity alone obscures the fact that many people fit more than one category. However, there are exclusion issues which have a particular bearing on certain marginalised groups. In the case of disabled children many of their parents want them to go to mainstream school; they see inclusion as a positive step towards social integration and becoming autonomous citizens.

To avoid the social underclass debate that gained political ascendancy in the Conservative years of the 1980s and 90s the government has introduced a number of policies that relate to children with special educational needs. Children with special needs other than physical also experience exclusion, such as those who have dyslexia. Gifted and talented children may find their education needs unmet so become bored, disinterested and restless in class, at risk of being labelled disruptive. This results in a high rate of economic inactivity and unemployment amongst people with disabilities. Some families can remember the stigma of being labelled retarded or backward because they had reading and writing difficulties. Bullock (1975) reports that the term slow learner was often felt to be a substitute for stupid. Africans with impairments suffer compounded discrimination.

6

The myth of race

Racialisation

Race is a relatively recent social concept, used by some to justify denying other people the same rights and freedoms as themselves.

Although the government mentions race inequality, the thrust of reforms continues to pursue colour-blind targets (Gillborn, 2001). When the influx of Caribbean African children into the British school system began in the early 1960s, there was no effort to prepare schools for the new population and the possibility that the old process of socialisation might be inappropriate for them. The new arrivals had not been through a primary school phase of acculturation and were completely unprepared for the level and nature of marginalisation they experienced because of their visible difference. They suffered rejection and verbal and non-verbal abuse. Racially charged demeaning terms were applied as labels of identification (Dhondy, 1985).

Marginalisation based on notions of race is a sophisticated and complex web of overt and covert meshes. To fully unravel it is beyond the scope of this book but even the social inclusion discourse serves to further marginalise and label those whom it seeks to include, for example, by using the term black (see chapter 1). The issue of race and negativity is a well-rehearsed discourse. The murder of Stephen Lawrence and, among others Anthony Walker, because of their colour, highlights the significance of race hate in society.

The Stephen Lawrence murder inquiry began in 1998 and the resulting report made 70 wide-ranging recommendations to eliminate the institutionalised racism they found (Macpherson, 1999). It implied that if the police and other services have been found to be institutionally racist, education and schools could well be the same. But there is no legislative obligation to implement any of the recommendations of the report. However, the Race Relations (Amendment) Act 2000 extends the scope of the 1976 Race Relations Act by placing specific duties on public bodies, including local authorities and schools, to be proactive in promoting race equality and to say how they will do this through their race equality policy.

Yet a Committee of Enquiry into the Education of Children from Ethnic Minority Groups, set up by the Government in 1979 and chaired by Anthony Rampton, had concluded that racism and its effects in school and society account in large measure for the failure of Caribbean African children in school. It pointed to intentional and unintentional racism and recommended that all who work with young people should become sensitised to the needs of the young people they work with so that they can develop positive attitudes to themselves in relation to world history.

The Rampton report (1981) called upon the government, the Department of Education and Science, the Inspectorate, Local Authorities, the Schools Council, teacher unions, examining boards, teacher training institutions and the Commission for Racial Equality to put the damage right. Interestingly, the committee subsequently underwent a change of chairman from Anthony Rampton to Lord Swann. The final report *Education for All* (Swann, 1985) asserted that under-achievement in schools, particularly among Caribbean African boys, is due to a variety of racial disadvantages.

More interestingly still, Swann chose to include a lengthy Appendix (p126-148) on the IQ Question (Mackintosh and Mascie-Taylor, 1985). These Cambridge academics make a laborious case to challenge the notion that IQ is related to race and that Black people are the least intelligent. But this idea had already long been discredited. They conclude that the reasons for differences in school achievement are due to social and economic factors and not 'genetic' factors.

Thus the race pluralisms in Swann are over-simplified and slip between description and prescription. It suggests that everyone should leave the margins which is neither inclusive nor a methodology for inclusive practice (Pring, 1978). The report echoed Lord Scarman's portrayal of a culture of deprivation (Bourne, 1994). 'Problem' children have continued to be a government concern, as evident from a spate of publications:

- 1992 Department for Education Discussion Paper, *Exclusions*

- 1993 Department for Education, *Pupils with Problems* Draft Circulars

- 1993 Office for Standards in Education, *Education for Disaffected Pupils*

- 1997 Office for Standards in Education, *Achieving Good Behaviour in Schools*

- 1997 Pupils with Problems Draft Circular No 3, *Exclusion from School*

- 2002 'Pupils with Problems Draft Circular No 4, *Education by LEAs of Children Otherwise than at School. (EOTAS)*

Not all ethnic minority groups experience the same degree of racial disadvantage and there is evidence that certain minority groups perform better in schools than white pupils. Chinese pupils obtain significantly higher attainment scores which, it is suggested, may be linked to issues of strong cultural identity (Thomas *et al*, 1994). So do Indian pupils, indicating that whilst class is a determining feature in attainment at school but that culture is also a factor.

Teachers' notions of cultural norms influence their expectations of young people. For example the prevailing broad stereotypes lead to expectations that young people of Chinese or Indian origin will be industrious, courteous and keen to learn. They are assumed to be well-disciplined, highly motivated and from backgrounds where educational success is highly valued. Whereas pupils of Caribbean African origin are expected to exhibit disruptive behaviour in class and are therefore more frequently reprimanded and controlled even when they are behaving like their white peers (Wright, 1992). The expectations attributed to excluded young people are often associated with crime, unemployment, drugs and deprivation. There is a tendency to conceptualise difficulties in behaviour and learning so that the student is seen as the one who has the problem (Fulton, 1993). This pathologising of young people, their families and their cultures is based more on media misrepresentation than on authentic rigorous research carried out by those affected by the labels.

British Caribbean African sub-culture is considered to be the main reason why the school process does not work (Sewell, 1997). However, quite the contrary is true: it is the sub-culture which sustains young people, giving them a feeling of belonging. Admittedly there are aspects of the sub-culture that are undesirable, as in any culture, but the sub-culture should not be an excuse to absolve the school system from responsibility to provide educational quality.

Cultural transference has been eroded in Caribbean African communities. As discussed in Chapter Two, a balanced world history has yet to be introduced in the mainstream school curriculum. Consequently, African diasporan collective self-knowledge has been arrested (Akbar, 1998).

Adolescence is a potentially difficult time. For disaffected adolescents this difficulty is often compounded by the apparent disregard by western society to meet their psychological, spiritual and social needs (Hill, 1992; Graham, 1999) or to instil a sense of self. Woodson (1996) argues that Africans should know their past in order to participate intelligently in national and global affairs. As we have seen, a strong sense of identity is a firm foundation for young people to build on in order to become productive citizens.

The British education system is failing African children in complex ways. One is the failure to introduce a full world history. Another is the failure to readdress the imbalance of negativity that bombards children with African heritage who underachieve in UK schools. Ofsted recognises that there is a discrepancy between what is being offered to young people and their needs.

Ofsted found that:

> Qualitative approaches reveal a considerable gulf between the daily reality experienced by many black pupils and the stated goal of equal opportunities for all. (Ofsted research, 1997, p55)

But it seems that penalties are imposed on pupils who raise issues of racism. Racial meanings change (Gillborn, 1987) and the insidious nature of racism is stealthy and felt mainly by those subjected to it.

Symbolic anti-racism is not the solution in the everyday world of real schools. Racism is difficult to prove and risky to not only the victim but also those who draw attention to it. Inappropriate curricula and teaching materials and the discouraging effect of socio-economic divides and poor employment prospects resulting from discrimination in the labour market, lead to marginalisation and exclusion (Rampton, 1981; Sewell, 1997).

Classification

The basis upon which the race argument takes place is flawed. Racism is based on a belief system that proposes that the human species consists of separate races, each with its own genetic and cultural features, that one race is superior to the others and that this false belief legitimises marginalising and discriminating against them (Wood, 2000). As science became established in the age of Europe's 'Enlightenment', racial classifications were assigned to people who shared a number of anthropological traits.

The distinguishing criteria of ethnic groups fall into two broad areas; genotypical and phenotypical, but neither relates to the capacity of humans to learn, and human beings all possess similar human genes regardless of classification. The similarity of all people at chromosome level is remarkably close.

Scientists have determined that the human species originated in the cradle of civilisation, Kemet (Ancient Egypt) in Africa. The oldest human discovered was an African female. Great African dynasties existed centuries ago. The evidence shows that there is only one human family so it is important to understand the origins of this disturbing classification of human beings.

Differentiation has a socially constructed agenda. What satisfies the socially constructed differentiating requirement is the phenotypical area of physical appearance such as colour. And that has been used to disparage people and undermine their cultural consciousness, knowledge systems and behaviour. Practices of discrimination are based on colour but colour is not the whole picture. Xenophobia, antisemitism, Islamophobia are all forms of racism by the dominant that drive discriminatory behaviour. Hostility is also based on differences of cultural representation in language and religion. So we have notions of cultural racism that are practice-based and symbol-based and colour racism which is visible. These physical and cultural markers of difference are lumped together to affirm and reinforce existing prejudice.

Ignorance about the importance of differentiating is at the heart of the inappropriate labelling of, interactions with and expectations of the dominated by the dominant. But the notion of differentiating by 'race' is scientifically invalid.

Pupils from minority populations are defined by their colour instead of by their culture as Africans, Egyptians, Arabs, Latinos, Asians, Pacific Islanders. Colour simply describes appearance but says little about people and their cultural norms.

The colour of racism

The cause of dark skin pigmentation is melanin (Browder, 1989), which protects the skin from the sun. Melanin darkens the skin and people became described in the colonialising process in the terms coloured, black and white. Africans have been described as coloured people, yet when bruised, Europeans are more likely to blush or go pale than Africans. If exposed to extreme heat or cold their colour response is more apparent, as when they are sunburned, severely chilled, shocked or embarrassed. And they called us coloured!

Because of colonial history, skin colour has placed Africans at a disadvantage. When they try to prove that they have been manhandled in school or elsewhere the melanin colouration of children camouflages injuries. But it does not stop the pain. When African people are embarrassed or humiliated their blushing is less visible. There is little concern about the ways in which they indicate discomfort. This resonates with the period of enslavement when African people were considered by the dominant to have no feelings.

Ignoring colour does not eradicate racism. We need instead to identify and remedy social policies that advantage some groups at the expense of others. Colour should be celebrated. As obvious as it seems, it should be acknowledged that all children have feelings. Continual cruelty towards children because they have less visible indicators to signal pain or humiliation should not be tolerated. An uninformed abuser can continue with a torrent of verbal attacks and not stop until they have satisfied what they believe to be a visual indication of subordination, which is a posture of dejection. Adult informants painfully recalled situations at school when a teacher, protected by school rules, psychologically beat them into submission.

> *They (teachers) used to shout right up in our faces in front of our friends that we should go home if we didn't like the treatment we received.* (Parent)

Looking at the unacceptable practice of categorising people as Caucasoid, Negroid and Mongoloid, we learn of the assigned characteristics and negative stereotypical labels which led to the arousal of subliminal anxieties (phobias). These conditions were described by Franz Fanon as Caucasophobic, Negrophobic and Mongolophobic (Fanon, 1967).

If practitioners who work with communities of visible difference hold subliminal phobias that make them perceive tall African boys as a threat, they will use their power inappropriately. Without self-awareness and self-development white teachers may not fulfil their duty to be inclusive and teach all students equally.

Education is value-based. Consequently, inappropriate labelling, interactions and expectations seriously disadvantage children's education, placing them at increased risk of exclusion. Although one can question whether value judgments are beyond scientific enquiry, such value judgments and their outcomes are not new and the exclusion of African people has taken place in a systematic and structured way in England over many years (Young, 1978). Marina Maxwell was the first to expose this prejudiced practice in schools in her article 'Violence in the toilets' (1966) followed by Bernard Coard in his book of 1971. Some educational providers, however, maintained that Caribbean Africans were ineducable.

Caribbean African and Asian children were considered to be underachievers because of their heritage. They were segregated in schools into lower streams or teaching bands (Bourne, 1994). This form of exclusion was based on prejudice, nourished by cultural and language differences. As we saw, many were declared educationally sub-normal on arrival from the Caribbean and placed in separate classes or bussed to separate schools (Coard, 1971).

The concept of race is no longer meaningful or even valid. We should instead be celebrating difference and working to remove labels. There is no evidence that children who are excluded or at risk of exclusion have a genetic disposition to exclusion or under-achievement. Nevertheless, whenever there is any mention of disaffection and excluded pupils, race and the term black surface because of the stereotypical negative discourse around underachieving African boys. My research indicates that it is teachers' cultural insensitivity, punitive approach and low expectations of African pupils that is contributing to much of the disturbing statistics of poor educational outcomes.

Culture

Definitions of culture can fall into the trap of a one size fits all approach, bestowing cultural attributes on groups, which are based on an outsider's understanding.

Africa has vast cultural diversity and is host to over 800 ethnic groups historically connected globally with cultures inside and outside the continent. No culture is static, timeless and only traditional. Cultures vary from region to region, among different ethnic groups, genders, language speakers, ages and classes in Africa, Europe, Asia, America, China and the Caribbean (Goggins-II, 1998).

Families and communities are important in every culture and society. They come in many different forms, so there is no one pattern to describe them. Families living side by side in the UK can have very different family situations and cultural practices. People and communities should represent themselves rather than being represented by a stereotype imposed by others. Difference should be seen as normal.

Within increasingly diverse third generation communities, children can become estranged from their cultural heritage. And they spend much of their waking hours with practitioners who are ignorant of their cultural norms and the high expectations held of them by their family and community. Some of these Caribbean African youth belong to a sub-culture of British pseudo-American culture that is far removed from the traditions of their forebears.

Asante (1988) argues that a hegemonic society uses societal institutions and resources to promote their own cultural heritage whilst devaluing all other knowledge-centred cultures through omission, distortion and misrepresentation. The perception of African youth in British society is seriously distorted by past and present racism.

There is no rigorous unbiased information about the intellectual or academic ability of young people excluded from school. Holding low expectations of marginalised groups indicates prejudice and prevents attention being paid to educational needs. If young people have needs which are unmet, they may develop survival behaviours which are considered disruptive or difficult to manage. Too often they will be classified as having emotional and behavioural difficulties (EBD) or behavioural emotional and social interaction difficulties (BES). Often it is racism that is the cause of such diagnosis.

If children's unmet needs are not investigated, they may be excluded by teachers who are unqualified to assess or diagnose their pupils or make appropriate educational choices on their behalf. Some exclusions originate from interactions between various teaching and non-teaching staff such as helpers who supervise young people during the lunch period and assume a role *in loco parentis*. Lunchtime involves large numbers of young people during concentrated periods of non-directed social activity in up to 16 percent of the school day (Wright, 1992).

When pupils are not afforded a professional diagnosis it is almost inevitable that any intervention will be inadequate, inappropriate and damaging. Without diagnosis the pupil's needs remain unclear. Routes into the category of disaffection are dangerously wide and can be based solely on prejudice and labelling, ignorance and incompetence. This results in the pupil being stigmatised and disrespected (Sewell, 1986).

Disrespecting an individual and their culture can undermine their self-esteem. For instance if staff persistently refuse to call a student by their first name and use their family name instead, they are ignoring an important aspect of their culture. In many cultures names have symbolic meaning (Goggins-II, 1998).

Persistent pathological undermining of young people as ESN, EBD, ADHD or SEN victimises them and compounds any already existing exclusion or labelling complex. It centres the problem on the child, creating a deficit view of them. Barrow (1986) maintains that if a child develops poor self-image at school, it is an indictment of the teachers. In other words, it is for teachers to take responsibility for their attitudes that precipitate the behaviours which lead to exclusion.

A non-threatening non-judgmental approach does not seek to blame but rather attempts to turn the focus away from the victim (Ryan, 1976). An approach is needed in which racism plays no part in exclusion.

Over the years one remedial programme after another has been directed at children. Current approaches to addressing issues associated with exclusions have included medication, such as Ritalin for emotional and behavioural problems like attention deficit hyperactivity disorder (ADHD). Such drugs, prescribed by clinical psychologists and health professionals, are highly addictive and it is still too early to determine if drugs prescribed in childhood may go on to be needed in adulthood. There is likely to be a symptomatic and diagnostic impact on employment and society at large because any hyperactive-impulsive tendencies induced by medication or ensuing drug dependency may affect long-term job prospects, thereby increasing vulnerability to further social exclusion of the already excluded.

My research reveals that young people are being labelled as disaffected at progressively earlier ages. Although mis-diagnosis is a risk, at least an assessment using established mechanisms would help in making informed decisions before automatically excluding and might result in a diagnosis which would reduce racist perceptions and provide the basis upon which to determine future education provision or other intervention.

Parents are often the only constant adults who have crucial information about the medical, cultural and family history of the child. Parental input into decisions taken at school is important for the following reasons:

- parents will usually have been involved throughout their child's life experience and therefore have continuity of perspective

- parents also have in-depth knowledge of the child

- parents are the coordinating link and can become active in a partnership and advocacy role. Professionals are bound by codes of ethics and the extent of their involvement is limited to the academic year they teach the child. Whereas parents are involved at every age and stage and can support effective transition between settings and life stages.

Despite the recent concept of parents as partners with schools, parents are not viewed as a professional component of a solution-focused intervention (Warnock, 1988). The 1981 Education Act, informed by many of Warnock's recommendations, gave legal backing to parental choice. It shifted the focus to look at the needs of the pupil and urged integration into mainstream schools and communities (Hill, 1997). This opened up special educational needs to a far wider population than before, but the 1981 Education Act was well meaning but toothless legislation because no one could enforce the recommendations made.

DfEE research published in 1998 indicates that intervention is most likely to be effective if the parents are fully involved (DfEE, 1998). But families can be uncertain of what to do if their child is excluded and in many instances they may be unaware that their child is even indicated by research to be at risk of exclusion.

Guidance
Although pupils, policy makers, schools, PRUs, projects and practitioners are offered guidance from codes of behaviour provided by their governing institutions or associations, parents are generally left out of the loop. This may be caused by lack of communication. No national standards or coherent guidance on such communication exist that are based on a thorough theoretical and practical foundation.

Numerous education projects operate throughout the UK. There is no national agreed standard for the purpose and nature of projects. Here we look at the history of education projects for excluded children.

I focused on the pedagogy and perspective of the practitioner to uncover the characteristics and requirements of social inclusion practice. My research found that some teachers are unable to engage with students because they are not culturally and community conscious. Teachers who do have cultural knowledge use the benefit of their insight and empathy to relate to their pupils.

The teacher's role in education is to facilitate their pupils' learning. This is highly dependent on interpersonal relationships. It requires sensitivity and the ability to listen to what young people say and to discern what lies behind their words, frowns and hesitations (Peters, 1975). In view of the changing trends in education there may be a case for reconstructing the teacher's role.

Teachers are regularly faced with new populations of students with widely varying needs in a society which is affected by global events. So how does the inclusive teacher or practitioner manage in this new climate? One way is for the practitioner to commit to a self-managed learning programme so that they are more confident and competent to meet the requirements of a changing learning population's cultural and knowledge needs. This may mean embarking on a programme of professional and personal development so that they can be more effective and professionally competent. This would create a form of fluency which is not only subject-based but subjective.

Conclusion

This chapter has considered racism and its effects on children who fall within the categories identified as at risk of exclusion and their families. A paradigm shift is required to resolve the problem of social exclusion as it relates to education. The approach to seeking solutions to excluding practices suggested here is that punitive policies have failed. Alternative practices are required.

As we decode the meanings of the historical and social shifts, what emerges is how certain sectors of society continue to exclude on grounds of race and class. They may change the language and the mechanisms but they still marginalise the groups they dominate, persisting with notions of us and them. Caribbean African children are often referred to as 'they', 'those children', 'these children' or as 'disaffected'. The people who have been labelled have so far had no voice. This research has heard the voices of young informants who reveal violations of human rights. Children are shouted at – if you walk through the corridors of many secondary schools you hear teachers hollering at students. Students and families speak of feeling humiliated and of being denied an opportunity to be all they can be, when they are marginalised and then excluded.

Racism has driven the differentiation of so called educationally subnormal (ESN) children, the denial of African history, the low expectations of African pupils, the confusion, lies and denial. PRUs have an unhealthy population of students who are contained, not educated. The mainstream school professionals often look down on the PRU professionals.

Exclusion is based on unequally applied rules of discipline and behaviour and referrals which are too often based on colour. Much of the
research indicates that punitive measures are harsher and more frequent for Caribbean African students.

> Sometimes singling out black students is done deliberately and oppres-
> sively. (Maud Blair, 2001)

7

A framework to support excluded pupils and issues around its implementation

I came to teaching to make a difference because I had such a hard time as a pupil myself. I didn't realise that I would get a hard time from my colleagues. Last term I intervened when a student was going to get excluded. Now they are not in the least supportive to me but I get my satisfaction from knowing I am helping children who would otherwise fail. (Teacher)

Overleaf is a diagrammatic representation of a model of socially inclusive practice. It is a holistic frame of reference model that can be used to underpin learning achievement and has eight key concept areas. Each concept has specific components related to the issues raised by practitioners. Together there are 32 components, which have been grouped into themes. This framework, or FORMULA, is effective because it is grounded in practice that works.

The key concepts of the model that emerged from the good practice observed in the study are:

- ▓ informed perception: how people in differing roles see things

- ▓ community alignment: the relevance of a service to the users

- ▓ communication: building on the social interaction which takes place between human beings

- ▓ collective concepts: objectives and the sharing of purpose and intention

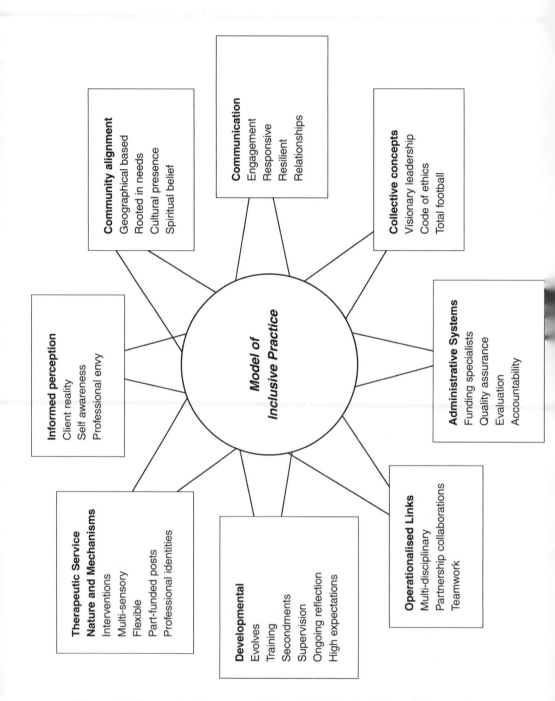

Figure 6.1: Frame of reference model underpinning learning achievement – FORMULA

- administrative systems: to provide the mechanisms for monitoring

- operationalised links: to provide good strong working networks that provide the inter-connection between agencies and individuals

- development: measurable progress is programmed into the service at all levels so there is a sense of advancement

- a service which is therapeutic in nature with mechanisms and pedagogies that do not penalise, exclude or marginalise.

These concepts form a framework for practice based on principles which can be applied in various service areas such as further and higher education, health, counselling, the probation service, social services, the police and the prison service. And they can be further developed to act as a training and development strategy, change agent, an inclusive practice measurement tool or a model of best practice.

Among the many issues raised by the informants in my research, the strongest themes that emerged concerned:

- client reality
- self awareness
- professional envy
- geographical location based in the community it serves
- provision rooted in needs of community it serves
- cultural manifestations
- spiritual belief
- engagement
- responsiveness
- resilience
- relationships
- visionary leadership
- code of ethics
- total football
- funding specialist provision
- quality assurance
- evaluation

- accountability
- multi-disciplinary professional teams
- collaboration in partnership
- teamwork
- evolving services
- training for practitioners
- secondments
- supervision
- ongoing reflection
- high expectations
- interventions
- multi-sensory approaches
- flexibility
- part-funded posts
- professional identities

These components feed into the eight key concepts in a seamless and integrated way. The dynamic of the various components is explained by giving examples of the components of inclusive practice and the perspectives of inclusion practitioners.

Client reality

Education professionals and practitioners must recognise that young people and their families may inhabit a world of conflict and urban deprivation which can limit their life experiences and opportunities.

In a climate of increasing violence, the exposure to drugs is ever present. Urban life for young people today is different from their parents' and teachers' own experience. The interviews conducted for my research were immensely revealing. One youth told me this:

> *And after school sort of – there was a fight. A big fight – a lot of people these two guys had tried to fight me and my friend. He hit my friend and then everyone sort of just joined in – that's fine – these two guys – they were like getting battered. Everyone was beating them up and after a while I was trying to stop it and no one was listening. The police come and everything and then, my friend's cousin, who was like 18 at the time, he was sort of sitting on top of one of them and hitting them. And, I*

grabbed him and got him off him. And he was just like going mad and everyone was – there was loads there – about twenty people trying to beat them up and then I grabbed one of them and said, come on let's go. And he was like, no, no, I'm not going. Like he was bleeding and I said, come on just let's go and then, he hit me. He hit me, he didn't knock me out but I couldn't get back up. I was hurt like. And then, the next thing I knew like, was all the teachers and the police like came and everyone just ran and left me and I got into so much trouble like.

So, it was all right. I didn't get into too much trouble. The police just like said, gave me a caution because the guy said like, I was trying to get him out of the situation sort of thing.

Inclusive practitioners are effective only if they move beyond their own reality and understand that the client's life circumstances may differ significantly from their own and that issues which affect the client will not affect the practitioner in the same way. The intention is to understand the person's lived reality and practitioners work towards not being shocked by what they tell them:

So, you know, I would speak to a student and I'd say, well okay, what is it you want to do as a career? Just a casual question that I asked. And, they would say, well my brother's a drug dealer. They get good money for doing that. I think I'll go down that route, you know. I said, mm.

So, obviously, when I first started I was kind of shocked by some of these statements. So, you know, you talk to people, trying to figure out what the hell is going on. But then, when I started doing the course, some of the stuff I learnt in that course helped me to deal with the stuff that came out in the lesson from the young people. (Rites Elder)

The young person's needs are kept uppermost whilst seeking a solution, in effect making the service client-centred rather than organisation-centred.

The biggest problem for me with the whole thing was that when schools decided to do this, it was about the school's needs quite often and not the young person's. The schools quite often felt that they weren't coping with the child, so put them on work experience, as opposed to the child feeling they need work experience.

So, after trying that for a while, which we thought was a really good model to work on and realising that quite often that kids were very re-

sentful about being there, rather than seeing the ... I mean, one of the things about inclusion initiatives is the young person must feel they want it. (Practitioner)

The data revealed the opinions of the inclusion practitioners held by the young people and their families. They spoke of practitioners in affectionate terms. They said they were 'nice' and spoke of feeling relaxed and calm with them, which implied that they might not feel that way in school. This suggests that teachers are not held in similar high regard. If teachers are the professionals young people encounter most in school why do young people not feel relaxed with them? Perhaps the teacher/pupil relationship needs exploring.

The children and their families communicated a strong sense of social justice. They related instances where they were supported or felt supported by inclusive practices. They made a definite distinction between what they think teachers do and what inclusion practitioners do. It appeared that teachers teach in a way that young people see as different from the way social inclusion practitioners interact with and educate them. One young person summed it up:

They're just – such nice people as well, Geraldine and all of them. Like, they will help with you with anything and they're just the sort of people that you need to know that there's people like that in life.

Because, teachers are just strict and, not all of them, but that's just the way they portray themselves because they have to, it's their job. But, these are just really nice people, like. I think it's a really good idea.

All the young people and their families spoke about the practitioners as a different category of educator than school teachers. One said:

Just like – they just sort of – they're like – they ... workers but it's not like they are. They're like – they're friendly. They're nothing like teachers or anything. They're sort of down earth. Really down to earth. And they understand where you're coming from sort of.

Another characteristic remarked on about the socially inclusive practitioner is how they provide an environment that is welcoming and conducive to learning. I talked with a Rites Elder, who told me:

One of the things that I notice a lot here is that people are – that the people who work in the office with us like, Tony and – and all of us really,

108

but I have noticed it a lot with Iris and with Cory, people in the office in which I work is that they're always very pleased to see them.

SR *Pleased to see them? Pleased to see who?*

PA *The students.*

SR *Sorry. You mean the staff are pleased to see the students?*

PA *Yeah. I do. And, I think that probably – I think that it's noticeable to me and I think it's quite an important thing. Because, it might not be what they get at school. Because, I think not because of schools or ... but because they're not set up that way. You can't – you know, teachers can't be individually pleased to see every single student. Do you know what I mean? I mean, you can't get that kind of – maybe they don't have it at home. I don't know.*

Inclusive practices start from a belief that behaviour is a symptom of unmet human need and that accepting the reality of the client may reveal the cause of the exclusion.

Self-awareness

To aid their ability to see the children they work with and their families' reality as distinct from their own, the inclusion practitioners undertake a programme of self-development. The data indicates how willing they are to raise their awareness of and then disengage from personal issues. They embark on a programme of self-development so they become better able to facilitate learning. And they work to help the children become self-aware too, so that they can make informed choices about their behaviour, peer pressure and what they want to achieve. A Rites Elder commented:

They learn a lot about themselves, you know. It's about, self-esteem stuff and about learning about yourself and learn who you are and let us learn as well, you know. Because, it is a learning establishment. It's a two-way learning establishment. You're not coming here to learn practical maths skills. And, we're here wanting to learn about you.

Mainstream practitioners confessed to witnessing disturbing abuses that led to their becoming committed to inclusive practice.

One of our teachers in High School abused the boys. He used to stand in front of boys from the Caribbean and tightly pinch the hair at their temple hairline gripping it between his thumb and finger and rotate. The boys would grimace but refuse to cry but they were clearly in pain. (Education Social Worker)

I went to a girl's school and one male teacher would stand at the side of girls and place one palm on the bottom of a girl and the other on her front privates while speaking to her. I used to be so scared. (Dinner Assistant)

Mainstream practitioners revealed in interviews that their school experience was characterised by low expectations, shattered dreams and stifled aspirations. A nursing lecturer said:

In the 70s my careers advice was that I shouldn't think of becoming a doctor but maybe become a clerk/typist or secretary. The boys were told they could become postmen.

Many inclusion practitioners believed in the value of a therapeutic approach, and engage in counselling, mentoring and coaching. They explained that failure to set aside unresolved personal issues would get in the way of being effective. This separating out of personal issues is fundamental. It contributes greatly to reducing the tendency to employ excluding behaviours. When a practitioner can recognise which of any of the issues that arise stem from their own unresolved problems and which are those of the pupil, they can work more quickly and appropriately to counteract barriers to inclusion.

The raised awareness of both themselves and their clients produces an environment where both can make informed choices about the roles and behaviours they will assume. It is an environment in which both parties are recognised as the holders of knowledge and as equally valuable contributors to successful inclusion.

Professional envy

The data revealed that some professionals may view others with disdain whilst at the same time believing they have access to lavish resources and conditions. A teacher seconded to a community-based inclusion initiative in order to gain insight into its practices told me:

This is such a luxury for anybody. And, it – I have to say, it galls me that the education service is paying for everybody to be here [doing professional development] on a Wednesday.

And, I won't say, messing about or playing, but teachers don't get this time. They don't have this luxury time. When I was teaching and having to write you know, maybe a letter home about a pupil, or four or five pupils, it would be done at 4.30 in the afternoon, you know. After everything else was done and the kids had gone.

Whereas, people here are able to clock up admin hours on a Wednesday, or whenever they like, you know, as part of their job. So much that goes on, on these Wednesdays that is an add on to any other teacher's life. But then, they're not all teachers and that's the other problem ... is trying to – I mean, I don't understand a Youth Worker's perspective. Or, a Counsellor's perspective, necessarily. I think, one of my jobs also is to get them to understand what a teacher's perspective is. And, what it is really like to be in a school, in a classroom.

Closely linked to perceived identity is professionalism of practice and respect for the professional identities of other professionals. This entails having the confidence to challenge other professionals who may privilege the restraints of budgets or performance tables over the interests of the pupils.

In addition to the issue of economics, the data revealed an unexpected dimension to the arena of social inclusion: envy. Evidence emerged that professionals who are supposedly working towards the same goal of inclusion and raising attainment for a pupil who is unplaced, excluded or at risk of exclusion, may be resented or viewed unfavourably by colleagues.

The seconded teacher quoted above conveys a mixed message: irritation and resentment, along with valuing having time to carry out administrative tasks during the working day whilst at the social inclusion project.

Feelings of disdain between professionals is not unusual but it can undermine co-operation between them. The joined-up thinking of the Every Child Matters agenda and the development of multi-professional disciplinary teams increases the likelihood of professional envy. Notions of inclusion, widening participation and aiming higher are all government-led initiatives which promote the ideology of collaborative working, yet there is no guidance on how to manage professional envy.

So how can inclusion can be offered to young people if the various professionals who are supposed to be working in the interests of these pupils find it difficult to work inclusively? The inclusive practitioners themselves often come up against barriers to success. They are working in a demanding and sensitive area where they too can be excluded or at risk of exclusion in the educational setting. They too may become marginalised.

I observed haughtiness in the demeanour of many school-based staff, unlike the modest interaction styles employed by the inclusive practitioners. Yet all have the same objective, which is to facilitate the inclusion of school children into education: only their qualifications differed.

The professional standing, qualifications and experience of inclusive practitioners is questioned by mainstream teachers and other professionals remarkably often. The matter of undermining inclusive practitioners requires further research. The qualifications of the various teaching professionals working in this field were relevant to my study.

An examination of the requirements for qualified teacher status indicates that a first degree and the learning of theories of learning and classroom-based teaching practice may be inadequate today. Student teachers must also satisfy the government requirement to pass the National Skills Tests in literacy, numeracy and information and communication technology (ICT) to reach professional standards. This can be done at some universities through a programme of theoretical modules and a professional tutor system with teachers in school acting as mentors during initial teacher training school-based placements. On successful completion, teacher trainees are recommended to the General Teaching Council for qualified teacher status (QTS).

Professionals with QTS receive pay on a scale that is higher than for qualified and experienced teachers without QTS. Other professionals also have weighted pay scales; this difference in pay can result in professional envy.

To be inclusive practitioners, professionals need to demonstrate not just academic qualifications but also emotional and social literacy and cultural competence. My data indicates that some of them are more highly qualified and experienced than the teachers because they have had specialist training at post-graduate level, in addition to wide practical experience both inside and outside school environments. They are also expected to exhibit personal qualities such as moral authority, interpersonal skills and a higher level of commitment than solely curriculum delivery and be willing to engage in ongoing professional and personal development. Unfortunately, they risk hostility from colleagues.

The way in which some mainstream teachers were seen to engage with pupils, their families and others showed no respect for the inclusive practitioners even when they were qualified professionals with specialist knowledge. Teachers often sought to attribute blame so that discussions were about fault, responsibility and accountability rather than about bringing the resources and experience of the professionals and partner agencies to bear on furthering inclusive practice.

Further research is required to examine the relationships between professionals and their impact on achieving inclusion. It is imperative to reduce the friction between mainstream teachers and staff who are not academically qualified but are effective inclusive practitioners. Unless the issue of professional envy is acknowledged and addressed, certain members of the same team may not feel confident in their interactions with colleagues. The responsibility for reducing this counterproductive behaviour rests largely with those who hold QTS and the widely recognised and accepted qualifications. Formal qualifications may afford a certain status in the mainstream arena but they do not equip teachers to carry out work of the level and nature required for achieving inclusion. An arrogant attitude towards colleagues is unhelpful and pupils can sense it.

Organisations and their operating systems have a responsibility to recognise the economic component of unequal reward systems. QTS staff may resent earning less than inclusive practitioners. So what happens is that inclusive practitioners go into mainstream schools and work with hard to reach pupils or provide education otherwise, and their specialised work may or may not be reflected in a comparative pay scale.

Such tensions cannot be overlooked when they spill into the classroom so that the practitioners exclude each other. Working in classrooms there may be students, teachers and teaching assistants, mentors, speech and language therapists, occupational therapists, parents and other helpers. The practice of excluding operates not just among children, who do this as part of their world, but also among practitioners. Young people are sensitive to all types of behaviour and social interactions, so how are they affected? And what if the impact on young people in terms of learning co-operation and generosity? Most importantly, how effectively can a team which is operating in this way achieve the agreed goals of raising achievement?

What too often happens is that a group of practitioners are each operating within their own concept of what socially inclusive practice is. With new partners regularly coming on board, attention needs to be given to the induction of strangers into the school. New practitioners are generally given no guidelines and know nothing about the prevailing practice. Visiting practitioners and teachers need to know the school rules and be aware of the possibility of professional envy and the mechanisms put in place to reduce, if not eliminate, excluding behaviours of all kinds. There must be procedures that ensure that practitioners new to the school do not have to deal with either overt abuse from pupils or covert abuse from colleagues.

Inclusive practitioners are specialists but the classroom teacher and parents are specialists too. The practitioner or parent who knows the history of the child may also be the one who cannot intervene in events which are contributing to the pupil's under-achievement. Relationships may have broken down, professional practice repertoire be exhausted and the situation out of control. A seamless transference and sharing of information and moral authority may be required, plus an agreed code of conduct between practitioners to reduce envious or arrogant behaviour and stay on task to foster social inclusion and achievement.

Geographical location

A feature of inclusive practice provision is its location. Pupils of the PRU are likely to become further labelled, when they have already experienced rejection from mainstream.

Inclusion services are sometimes situated off the high street in areas designated suitable for regeneration. Situating a service like this in the daunting offices of the borough council can dissuade potential clients from using it.

Provision rooted in the needs of the community it serves

Inclusion initiatives aim to provide education otherwise than at school for a population of unplaced and excluded pupils who are vulnerable to excluding practices. The service interventions are designed to meet the particular needs of the excluded pupils. This ensures that the service is rooted in the needs of the young people and their families rather than application of a nationally directed 'one size fits all' approach. Inclusive practitioners are expected to work in a structured way in unstructured social contexts. This requires a high level of competence guided by an informed but not rigid approach.

Cultural manifestations

Diversity is evident in the cultural profile of the children and their families, practitioners and the wider community. Traditional garments are worn by some of the young people, their families and the practitioners. The inclusion service must demonstrate recognition and respect for different cultural norms that extends far beyond cultural days, the celebration of cultural festivals or African history month.

Practitioners need to be seen in the community they work in. Their work will include going into schools, youth centres, colleges and even the local fast food outlets that pupils often frequent. Although some practitioners drove to work, they made an effort to walk around in the community and to buy from local shops. An adolescent told me about a taster day:

> SR *So, your head of year in London High suggested you go to the taster day and you just went along?*
>
> M *Yeah.*
>
> SR *Why did you go along?*
>
> M *Because, it was like – it was at like 12 o'clock in the day sort of and they said we'd have lunch and everything. So, it was getting out of school. Get out of school.*
>
> SR *Okay. Cool. And then what happened on the taster day?*
>
> M *Bruce spoke to everyone and told us what it was about.*
>
> SR *Was there a lot of people there?*

M   *Yeah, there was quite a few. Yeah, from different schools. And then like, they put us into groups and sent us off like, with different people doing that. We had this Tony and he was doing the music and we spoke to him about that. And then, we went to like, different rooms and stuff in a group, so we got to know other people and then we got to know a whole lot of teachers but they weren't at the same time like. And it was good, like. And everyone was like, they were all friendly and everything.*

SR *Who were friendly?*

M   *All the workers. They were all smiling like and being nice to everyone sort of thing. A different atmosphere than I'm used to. That I was used to, so it was like – I liked it more because it was less tense. Just like – the way they were made you feel relaxed. That's how I knew that ... school and stuff because ... down to earth sort of thing.*

SR *How old were you then?*

M   *I was like 15 nearly 16.*

SR *So, how old are you now?*

M   *16 still, but 17 next month.*

SR *So, it was something you weren't used to? The atmosphere was different from what?*

M   *From that. Because at school we're sort of – where I live – I live like on an Estate, that's quite rough. So, I'm not used to people like – people you don't know coming up to you and saying, hello and introducing themselves and that.*

SR *Is that what they were like?*

M   *Yeah. Wah!*

Inclusive practitioners undergo a programme of anti-discrimination awareness training and learn to value cultural differences. This anti-discriminatory approach informs decision-making meetings, events, literature, images, refreshments (vegan, halal or kosher). Training is provided to minimise the misunderstandings that arise as a result of the misinterpretation of non-verbal behaviour, dress habit, hair, clothes and behaviour patterns. This is carried to the pupils, as they told me:

> *Well, we just all had our total different backgrounds, like. That we had all come together and talk about them, like, eventually.*

116

First of all, we weren't. And then, they take us on trips and things and they just make us relax more really.

Spiritual belief

The practitioners acknowledge the belief systems of all people including those new to England and to British culture; this is apparent in subtle symbols of spirituality, evident in spoken and unspoken language and in the use of in the use of images which recognise different faiths. A Rites Elder said:

> *We're providing a framework for education for students, who are all excluded students with quite heavy emotional needs, behavioural problems and family work. We concentrate on them and provide education as well as the support for that.*

> *And then, we've got the refugees and asylum seekers and those displaced and they get a similar service, concentrating more on their needs of integration. Helping them with housing, ID cards, all those kind of things are related. It's a bit of a challenge.*

Another fascinating revelation of the data is the widespread acceptance of spirituality. This acceptance of an unseen force in the world of work that is not driven by religious dogma is evident in informal conversations. It was evident that a higher power is recognised that is not strictly about religion or spirituality. It is about the things that cannot physically be seen, things that operate on a metaphysical level. For instance a belief that things do not happen by accident but by divine intervention and synchronicity. Things that operate on a metaphysical level are given just as much importance as those that happen on a metaphysical level.

> *I love the work we do with our students. Don't get me wrong, it's not a piece of cake by any stretch of the imagination but all of us know we couldn't do any other work it's what I've been searching for. I have this feeling I've been training for this all my life and ... I dunno.*

> *Somehow when we can't work things out like where we're going with this or that or money. Things work themselves out. We know we are doing important spiritual as well as education and employment work. In fact I think everyone who works here would say they feel like they want to come to work because of the difference we make and not the money we get.*

Engagement

A critical objective for the inclusive practitioner is engagement. One Rites Elder described how engagement might be established.

I'm Grant. You're – because, I know it's easy with someone I know, you know. I just give them my card at first. I say, give us a bell when you're ready. Or, I'll ring you next week. I mean, I've never met kids who said, tell me to Fuck off. Yeah, yeah man, all right, you know.

There's a kid I started working with two years ago, when I first started, about 18 months ago, Tom. Everyone really, well, from the schools, everyone. And, I wasn't in his face. Now he's on the refresh start. He's one of the best attenders they've had. Well, where's that come from? It's come from us. Just being there and knowing that – I'll come back again. And, that's what I do. I go in the chicken shop and I'll wave at someone. Or, you are – you know, just introduce myself. And, I've got a pack that I sell to everyone. So, I – every kid I meet. I'm not a Social Worker. I'm not a teacher. I'm not a Social Worker. I'm not a teacher. What I think I am, is a nosy bastard and I just want to know. You can tell me whatever you want. And, that's the first thing I always say to them. Because, the first thing they'll say to you, what, are you a teacher? I think you must be a Social Worker. No, I'm not one of them either. Or, a Truant Officer, they still know, you know. Kids use terminology of 10 years ago, Truant Officers, you know.

You go round to the Police and pick us up when we bunk off. I say, no, I don't think so, you know. I explain to them. I try to explain what I do.

SR *And, you say what?*

I say, I'll try and help you. I'll try and support you to get you through to tomorrow. They say, what do you mean by that? I say, well do you know what you're doing tomorrow? A lot of them say, yeah, I'm going to the park. And I say, what can happen to you in the park? What will you be doing? What do you mean? Well, when you go to the park, what do you do, do you just sit there? Play football? Then they give you the bravado, you know, oh we smoke squiffs or whatever.

For what reason? What do you mean, for what reason? Because, we do. Don't you ever smoke? No. So, I don't know why you do it. And then, I think I've got a skill in, you know, we generate conversation.

The subtleties and patience required to engage such young people can be demanding. Socially inclusive practitioners have to be confident and competent enough to engage with the child or adolescent and establish human engagement with them without the clinical pressure of strict time frames. Sometimes simply being there and establishing rapport is the priority, whether in a climate of enjoyment or discipline. One pupil said:

> *I found it – I did. Because I felt like, they didn't have to do that for me. Do you know what I mean? They actually made the effort to come all the way down to London High School, even if it was just down the road. But, they didn't have to come and see my teacher or see my form tutor, do you know what I mean? And tell them what's happening. And she did that and I thought, that from there, I knew that – that's when I started getting committed to the meetings. And I came all the time.*

Once rapport has developed, young people and their families feel they can initiate contact:

> *So, I think they're just exceptional people, Geraldine and that. They're just genuinely nice people and you couldn't train to do a job like that. Because, I could go and talk to Geraldine or any of them, about anything.*

Responsiveness

Inclusive practitioners offer a service that is responsive because of the work they have done on increasing awareness of their own personal issues. Responsiveness is distinctly different from crisis management: it allows the practitioner to respond quickly to issues which are a real feature in the world of young people, such as gangs, drugs, assaults and even murder.

With such issues daily affecting young people's lives, the practitioner has to be able to respond with cultural competence and sensitivity, moral authority and social capital which means a combination of skills that earns their trust and respect. They have the ability to respond appropriately and swiftly in a way that is not restricted by bureaucracy, is not too heavy or too light handed and which sensitively avoids disclosure. This requires an approach that doesn't violate confidences and avoids causing embarrassment or undermining teaching professionals, who may have difficulty appreciating the far-reaching consequence of excluding behaviour. This balance between rules of bureaucracy and the rules of community respect is one of the special strengths of inclusive practitioners. Their responsiveness enables them to recognise the needs of both the teachers and the pupils and to respond flexibly and humanely. One Rites Elder put it like this:

> It's not interventions. It's not the courses. It's not the mentoring. It's not anything else. It's just them feeling they can be engaged. That someone will respond to them, in terms of what they need. Won't let them down.

Resilience

Resilience is a constant feature of inclusive practice. One inclusive teacher gave a revealing insight into his personal commitment:

> I'm shattered some times, frustrated, I go home crying, I'm done. I get up in the morning and I'm eager to come back. And, what it is, is because, on a personal level, I feel I've found something that I've been looking for. As a Youth Worker I've always wanted to help young people and support them and be there for them. This Project does it on a bigger scale. Because I meet different kids every day of the week.

Inclusive practitioners balance patience with instilling certain values into the young people they work with. A Rites Elder related one exchange:

> Now, one of the examples I could use is, a student said to me the other day, what happens if I'm late to your class, you know. So, he is in a College environment and I said, well, one I won't be happy that you're late. But, for another, you'll miss whatever is happening, for starters. It will go on your record that you're late, yeah? I'll have to phone the school to say, well, dah, dah was late, came half an hour late, or 15 minutes late.

> If then also, if you're continuously late you then start to set a trend that people associate you with lateness, yeah. Those are the sort of things that would happen. And then, I talked about the repercussions later in life, if you go to College. ... they say, you know what, don't come back. Or, if you've got a job, they may give you one chance, two chances, ten chances but there may come a point when they say, you know what, don't come back, yeah. So, these are the sort of things that could happen if you're continually late.

> So, I tried to kind of explain it out. So, he said, okay. And then I said to him, okay, what happens at school if you're late? He said, well if you're

*late at school, you get detention. That's it. No one really ... Right, stay in
after school for half an hour and that's it.*

*So, I'm trying to do things slightly different and give them a different way
of looking at things. All things which will benefit them in the future.*

Practitioners need to be very resilient because young people who have
been rejected can develop ways of protecting their feelings which could
be anti-social. They may refuse to co-operate, they may have difficulty
in articulating their arguments. If professionals they once trusted have
disappointed them, their attitudes, behaviour and language might
appear hostile.

Inclusive practitioners may also need resilience to deal with professional envy from their teaching colleagues and their assertions that the
pupils, even though they attend school regularly, don't want to learn.
People make choices and if a child is turning up at school one could de-
duce that they do want to learn. It is therefore incumbent upon the
teachers to teach them. The greater the challenge, the more skilful the
professional needs to be.

Openness and persistence are characteristics of resilience. I observed
young people being constantly reassured that the practitioner will be
there for their benefit and not be judgmental. Being readily available
and maintaining a progressive approach requires simultaneously establishing boundaries and mutual respect. If this is accomplished, discussions about the consequence of behaviours and inconsistent
attendance are longer seen as threatening:

One youth worker spoke for all in demonstrating the persistence the
inclusive practitioners need:

*They gave me a list called a hard to reach list, which the borough used
to have. And, by the end of it, I contacted – I had contact with every single
one. And, that's because, is it because I'm persistent? It is because of
my approach.*

*It was by persistence and by not being in the kids' faces, you know, I
eventually saw ... Most of them I ended up seeing in Court. I went to –
one of my jobs ... I went to London Magistrates Court, I think, on about
49 occasions last year, with different kids. And, I eventually learnt that if
I was there on a Tuesday morning, I would see three or four kids that are
on my list.*

Relationships

The success of the approach to inclusive practice hinges significantly, although not entirely, on relationships. The flexible and responsive nature of therapeutic intervention must work through the complex nature of relationships. Practitioners who are comfortable and confident in their interactions with young people demonstrate a high degree of emotional literacy (Majors, 2001).

An inclusive practitioner observed:

> *A lot of people talk about communication being difficult. And for me, the most important things that have made this work are the communication and the relationships.*

Students echo many of the sentiments of inclusive practitioners. One said:

> *This place is the best place, I reckon. Yeah. If you have problems, you can just sort it out here properly. And, they're all friendly people and you wouldn't have any problems with any of them.*

Relationships between colleagues are also valuable. They provide the insights from other disciplines but, more importantly, practitioners can draw on the professional expertise of another discipline such as psychotherapy, social services or the police. As one put it:

> *Because, a lot of the kids are kids who are not attending school. Who are being out of school etc, or being disruptive in school, are not engaged. So, the essence and I think the thing that – when I look at the staff here that I feel really comfortable with, is how well they – and how quickly they can engage with young people. How quickly they can develop a trusting relationship.*

Children are sensitive and receptive to the kind of authority which is based on mutual respect and social justice. Such a relationship brings with it moral authority. Practitioners and the pupils and their families are guided by trust and an agreed code of conduct. The practitioner operates in a way that is not authoritarian but authoritative, a type of parental moral authority to which children respond positively. This moral authority is exercised in the interactions between young people and practitioners and enhances the communication. Potential confrontations are resolved by unspoken interactions between them. Dur-

122

ing the three-year study, I heard only one shouting incident and that was during boisterous play in a recreation period. No inclusive practitioner shouted at any time during my research. My experience in schools was, as I have noted, entirely different.

Visionary leadership

The philosophy of inclusion is that all young people deserve a chance and should not be written off. The government's consultation document *Aiming High: Raising the Achievement of Ethnic Minority Pupils* (2003) identifies one of the characteristics of a successful school as strong leadership. Inclusive practice leadership is strong and the practices are based on the principles and ideology underpinning the spiritual framework of *MA'AT* as well as four therapeutic models used in counselling. These counselling models are humanistic, psychodynamic, cognitive behavioural and multicultural.

MA'AT promotes the practice of truth, reciprocity, balance, righteousness, peace and justice. Good leadership enables and empowers staff by being accessible and supportive. Development meetings and supervision are regularly held with inclusive practitioners. Working practices are shared by shadowing and informal discussion. Inclusive practitioners I interviewed recognised that even though difficulties may exist, it was the leadership that facilitated a climate of inclusion.

> *And yet, I've found a Project Manager that I think actually gets the balance right between you know, boundaries, statutory safeguards and a kind of open access.*

Code of ethics

Inclusion has an ethos and a code of ethics. Responsibility, respect and confidentiality are based on strongly humanitarian themes such as human rights, equality, fairness and advocacy. The commitment to reaching out into the community is demonstrated by outreach activities. Working practices are shared by shadowing colleagues from other disciplines and informal discussion in social contexts to gain insight into rules that govern the practice of other professionals. For instance, a teacher may shadow a social worker to get an insight into the perspectives that might govern or influence the actions other social workers.

Total Football

SR *Is there anything else that you think it would be useful for me to know?*

Elder *Just think Total Football.*

SR *Total...?*

Elder *Total Football. We play every position.*

Understanding Total Football means being open to a new theory of flexible space and practice, to wrap your mind around the idea that football isn't merely a sport. It is a practice based on position-switching: which substantially reduces the repetitive pillar to post experiences of the excluded.

The philosophy of Total Football was evolved by Dutch football coach Rinus Michels. It is defined in the online encyclopedia *Wikipedia* as

> ... a system where a player who moves out of his position is replaced by another from his team, thus retaining their intended organisational structure. In this fluid system no footballer is fixed in their intended outfield role... Total Football depends largely on the adaptability of each footballer within the team to succeed. http://en.wikipedia.org/wiki/Total_Football

Total Football happens in educational inclusion when you combine joined-up humanitarian ethics with professional service delivery. It is about getting results that significantly improve the school learning experience for students, families and the practitioners.

In this approach it is the team and not the individual professional who attains a win-win with the pupil and family. There is no blame culture and no competing. A Total Football prerequisite is willingness to accept both individual responsibility and team tactical aspects, and to maintain a positive attitude towards colleagues and the student. There is little rhetoric: success lies in the doing and the willingness to do. The team leader recognises when things are going wrong by having an idea of what it's like when things are going right. The plan of operation is based on the collective vision and understanding of a seamless team approach to service delivery.

In the context of education Total Football is based on a concept that transcends notions of teamwork. The concept is based on the belief that the rigid boundaries of professional role identities should not restrict

124

service delivery to the client. Although originating from a sport-based concept, it is transposable into professional practice, which can be seen in action on a daily basis. The pupils' aspirations are the focus and where necessary they are passed seamlessly to colleagues to ensure that their needs met. I witnessed productive discussions between colleagues about how to facilitate a student's needs rather than hand them over as caseloads to external professionals.

Total Football is an organic approach to working with young people. Basically, the objective is to score a goal from whatever position you hold or play. In this fluid system an unavailable professional is replaced by another from the team. No professional is fixed in their primary role; anyone can temporarily be a point of contact and ensure that service provision is maintained. Inclusive practices are encouraged to provide a seamless service so that if a client turns up unexpectedly hoping to see their allocated contact, someone can be there for them if the person they had hoped to see cannot. They deal with the needs of the client and update the relevant practitioner on their return.

Funding specialist provision

Successful inclusion initiatives require unravelling the maze of funders, funds, funding opportunities, language, project proposals and responding to government policy. Funding affects staff recruitment and retention funding. The constant scramble for funding is creating a climate of stress and insecurity. The efforts that go into funding applications are a serious drain on resources and long-term planning. Funding rounds, government agenda and policy language require the attention of a funding specialist.

Quality assurance

Quality assurance requires regular meetings to examine the nature and quality of the interventions being operated. The systems administrator works with the team to design forms and computer systems to record features and feedback of clients, partners and rites elders. Maintaining a service of high standard is one of the dimensions of inclusive practice provision.

Evaluation

Evaluations are a snapshot in time. They show how far you've come and give you an idea of how far there is to go. Any service provider worthy of the name must evaluate (Rossi *et al*, 2004).

Evaluations can be objective or subjective. An objective evaluation requires some form of measurement so that achievements are quantified and measurable. Subjective evaluations are valuable as they offer the opportunity to hear the voices of the respondents. However, they may be anecdotal and so not offer the same clarity in terms of a particular phenomenon – and these may be difficult to ratify. But they do need some standards in place to serve as a measure. The criteria must be meaningful, valid and consistent. It must be established how the criteria will be measured to ensure consistency.

Projects often carry out evaluations which are relatively straightforward using statistical information. However, qualitative evaluations are required too, as they can identify strengths and areas for further development.

Accountability

Community-based service providers may not be governed by the same legislation as schools and PRUs, which are accountable to the DCSF. However, there is a requirement by the stakeholders for community service providers to be evaluated also even though they are not accountable to the DCSF. In addition, local authorities who retain the statutory obligation to ensure that young people receive an education are required to ensure that all service providers make available suitable education to the young people placed with them. This is the goal of the inclusion service providers.

Multi-disciplinary professional teams

A teacher explained the make up of the socially inclusive team she formed part of:

> *We've got therapists, youth workers but the good thing as well, which I think is really important you know, you can't just have youth workers, teachers, social workers, in a service like this. You also need artists. You need musicians. You need cleaners that come in and have a laugh with us and the kids and you know, it has to be inclusive as well.*

So, you know, that's really important. So, it's got all these people in these different roles that can respond in different ways to young people. With, possibly one of its weaknesses, not a great deal of structure around that. But, that's great because we can respond flexibly.

Having a team with some insight into how other disciplines and organisations work is particularly important when dealing with a client group whose needs can be extremely complex.

Partnership collaboration

Collaborations are important at every level and teams need to work together to establish external inter-agency links so that young people and their families feel safe, cared for and respected. The external links cannot be as intimate as the links within teams, but are vital. Inclusion practitioners believe that success lies not simply with theoretical links but in positive working links. This is made possible by openness, sharing knowledge and forming forums and platforms for synergy.

With one of the Senior Behaviour Team actually ... we set out to go and reach all these kids, or try to. And, you know, touch wood, she was really good. She did all the???, we now call ourselves, the good, the bad and the ugly, you know. Because, she has her remit. I think she really cares for the kids she works with and between me and you and 25 million people, I think she's the only one in the Senior Behaviour Team that's got that ability.

Teamwork

Inclusion initiatives create strong multi-disciplined teams of professionals with good working internal links between those in the same team. These teams may have different areas of responsibility – supervision, training, finance or strategy. Cross-fertilisation nurtures the team, consolidates the broader teamwork and promotes the strengthening of different areas of the organisation.

...we never come in to see a situation or young person and think we have the answers. How we approach it is, always, let's find out together. We also think it's a long-term thing. It's not about; this kid's got a drug problem. It's not that – got a drug problem, got a family problem, you've got peer problem, they've probably got a learning difficulty ... We never approach it as, this one's got this and concentrate on that. It's never – we don't feel that, we as human beings are that simplistic. We think things are inter-related. Our approach is always quite holistic. We try and investigate everything. And, everything is quite individual...

The way in which the inclusion team operates can make it difficult for outsiders to locate where accountability lies. This does at times create difficulties. As one frontline service provider observed:

I'm saying there's a lot of – there's too much interlinking. Because, of what Cory does. What Bruce does? Who they represent? I don't know who they represent.

Evolving services

Inclusion initiatives seek to build to capacity as they evolve to meet the service delivery needs of a changing client group. They were originally formed in response to the increasing issues affecting children who were excluded from school-based mainstream education to provide education otherwise than at school so they could still access education and training. They adapt to the current situation and legislative agenda by being informed by the needs of the pupils and not just by the agenda of the DCSF.

Training for practitioners

Training includes anti-discriminatory practice, alternative worldviews and disseminating good practice to eliminate the practices which exclude. Inclusion centres are involved in the internal training of staff to provide training and internment to other professionals and in feeding into the training programmes of other organisations. In addition they continue to explore new ways to develop the practice of the professionals and enhance their cultural and inclusive competence. As one Rites Elder remarked:

And, the training opportunities allow me to progress as a human being. Not as a professional, because you know, the training we do is about being human, I feel.

Secondments

An objective of inclusion is to share good practice. This is done in a number of ways, including conferences, training and secondments of professionals from other agencies and by providing social inclusion Rites Elders to work with other organisations. In this way they demonstrate and disseminate good practice in various settings and social contexts.

Supervision

Practitioners are supported and supervised at every level with guidance, opportunities for practice reflection and revised action planning. Supervision of this kind is not to be confused with line management or appraisal; it originates from the discipline of therapies such as psychotherapy and counselling. Trained professionals also provide clinical supervision to colleagues where it is deemed worthwhile. This ensures that practitioners do not become embroiled in the issues that affect their clients to a degree that they become ineffective.

Ongoing reflection

Young people and their families may have access to a variety of interventions which are employed by inclusion initiatives and are dependent on their individual needs. Determining the most appropriate course of action depends on continual reflection. Practitioners are encouraged to reflect on their practice and consider ways in which it could be developed to ensure that the most appropriate intervention is determined for each child. This approach requires an appreciation of delayed gratification and the patience to invest in the child. Through later reflection the practitioner considers whether they have done enough and could do more to ensure that their needs and their family's needs are met.

High expectations

Socially inclusive practitioners are encouraged to have high expectations of the young people they engage with and to offer them encouragement and recognising their achievements. This is a characteristic which is identified in a successful school and presented in *Aiming High: Raising the Achievement of Ethnic Minority Pupils* (2003).

Multi-sensory approaches

The inclusive practice provides a service which recognises the existence of sensory intelligences such as creativity, intuition, feelings, enthusiasm, empathy and reflection. These are drawn upon to assist in engaging with pupils and their families, colleagues and other individuals involved in providing education to pupils who are excluded or at risk of exclusion.

Flexibility

As well as being responsive, inclusion initiatives seek to be flexible. A number of different external agencies have commented on the flexibility of the service. One feature of its flexibility is that availability is not restricted to classroom learning or within school hours or only from 9 to 5.

> *I mean, it's more than clinical in a sense that we are much more flexible as to the things we say. I mean, our boundaries are less rigid, I think, that we would go – I mean, I think there's a culture here that people go out of their way to achieve something, literally.*

> *I mean, if something needs to be done we will make sure that it's done, that's the sort of way we think you have to work.* (Youth worker)

> *This is my main role, but you know, for want of a better way of explaining it, like I said everything that we have a thing about personal development. And, that means empowering levels, flexibility. We have our specialist areas but we ... people to drift across. So, somebody will call me and say, I'm working with a primary pupil, I think you will have a good relationship with him. I want you to engage them. I will go and do a family visit with them, or do one to one with the child. Or, if I need to go on a residential you know – it's flexible enough that I can do other things.* (Rites Elder)

Part-funded posts

Flexibility in the way inclusion initiatives are set up encourages the sharing of practice by providing a system of part-funding posts. Any position in a social inclusion team can be funded by two or more organisations. In this way inclusive practitioners can share their time and the inclusive practice approach with more than one organisation at a time.

Professional identities

Practitioners recognise the confusion over how others see them and how they see themselves. The dilemma of maintaining a professional identity relative to their particular background discipline becomes apparent in the multiple identities they adopt when interacting with school-based teachers.

Returning to the diagram on page 104, it is clear that a great many conditions need to be met if we are to construct a framework for supporting excluded pupils and those at risk of exclusion.

8

How educational providers can achieve inclusive practice

To recover and restore humanity the world must also be viewed through the eyes of people disaffected as a result (of enslavement). Part of the process is a relaying of history in a balanced way and establishing African intellectual structures to deal with the plight of African descendants. This is hampered until Ancient Egypt is recognised a classical civilisation and the intellectual foundation of Africa in the same way as the Greeks serve as the intellectual foundation of Europe. (Cheikh Anta Diop)

How inclusive practice affects pupils and their families

Periodically I submitted qualitative evaluation forms to the children who were the targets of inclusive practice and their families. Analysis of these forms indicates that there is:

■ positive change in pupil attitudes to learning and working hard

■ improved retention of knowledge

■ beneficial knock-on effects or chains of reaction into general social and education processes such as relationships, behaviour, peer monitoring

■ motivated and improved attendance

Framework transferability

The framework for inclusion practice on page 104 can be used in statutory organisations, the private sector and community-based social enterprises, national or international and of whatever size. Should the model appear to be difficult to transfer in its entirety, its valuable capacity to separate out the service provider from the pupil concerned can be emulated. The model can work with all school pupils, not only those who are unplaced, excluded or at risk of exclusion.

Adolescence is a time of confusion, rapid physical changes intense feelings and fluctuating emotions. Accordingly, working with teenagers requires sensitivity to such changes. Teenagers are not adults (Sewell, 1997) and require help and support to get through these stages towards adulthood. Traditional cultures, whether Jewish, Asian, American Native Indian or African, have used rites of passage ceremonies as a marker for cultural socialisation. Such culturally-based rites of passage offer a successful anthropological approach to the process of socialisation.

We must accept that some of the causes of stress in our target group's lives are likely to be school exams, coming to terms with their sexuality, abuse (psychological and physical), violence, bullying, being bereaved of their peers and self-harm. They live with the persistent onslaught of racial discrimination and the effects of a western value system which is oppressive in terms of class, race, gender, disability and sexuality. All these factors create a need for alternative paradigms that can meet the needs of all children as they grow up, and reduce the possibility of excluding behaviour being used as a punitive tool.

What platform is there for the child who feels unfairly treated? What are people expected to do with emotions like anguish, confusion, tears and anger that they were never allowed to express as schoolchildren? Without a platform for them all to voice their concerns and be heard, the school experience can become traumatic.

The existing models are ethnocentric. Scholars such as Asante (1988), have argued for the need to explore alternatives. It is difficult for Eurocentric models to be adapted to the way in which African people come to know and create knowledge. And Eurocentric models tend to universalise or dominate. Learning is experienced differentially and local conditions and opportunities influence that experience.

Research by Ofsted found that:

> African Caribbean young people, especially boys, have not shared
> equally in the increasing rates of achievement; in some areas their per-
> formance has actually worsened. (Ofsted, 1997:78)

Leading psychologists of African origin such as Na'im Akbar, Wade
Nobles and Amos Wilson introduce African-centred ways of knowing as
the framework for helping construct new paradigms. Their emphasis is
on the interconnectedness of physical, mental and spiritual aspects of
people's being (Wilson, 1992). This contrasts dramatically with the
existing hegemony that proposes that Eurocentric models of philosophy and psychology can be applied universally for all people in all
cultures.

Worldviews are culturally determined. This research showed how the
mindsets and different understandings of the human psyche that had
been dismissed, marginalised, or deemed primitive can be used to offer
a cultural contextualisation more relevant to people from different cultures (Myers, 1988; Akbar, 1976).

Research by Edwards *et al* (1998) suggests that in order to equip people
with knowledge and skills which support their active participation in
their own development and in view of cultural shifts, we should look toward new forms of social learning. African adolescents experience the
challenges common to their age group, plus the consequences of hostility, oppression and concealment of their history, and this is further
compounded by the apparent failure of western society to meet their
psychological, spiritual and social needs (Hill, 1992; Graham, 1999).
They face discrimination and low expectations and are constantly bombarded with derogatory images of themselves in popular culture. As
Graham (1999:260) rightly says:

> The transition of young black people into adulthood is particularly fraught
> within British society ... Many young black people have been indoc-
> trinated by the street culture that is encouraged by the media and viewed
> by society as black culture.

Traditionally, African scholars and researchers have been locked into
Eurocentric paradigms in shaping the frame of reference for black experience. However, respected African centred academics advocate an
alternative paradigm that affirms the traditions and customs of African
people, locating them at the centre of analysis rather than as objects of
existing frameworks (e.g. Karenga, 1990; Diop, 1978).

Margaret Donaldson (1986) observed that if teaching doesn't make human sense it is ineffective. Human sense is determined in part by cultural and social relationships. Placing human sense at the centre of teaching and learning requires an approach that considers the student's cultural and social experience and is prepared to develop multi-disciplined partnerships. This holistic and student centred approach to raising achievement places equal opportunities and social inclusion at the core of its practice.

Rites of passage

I knew that if I could get young people from Britain to learn about their history and culture first hand they would embrace their African cultural heritage. (Rites Elder)

Rites of passage programmes advocate what is termed a learning society and offer an empowerment curriculum which values the potential of the individual (Ranson, 1992). It seeks to instil positive attitudes and self-esteem among students. In addition, the purpose of the programme is to reinstate a system which re-introduces and validates cultural heritage and identity.

Western societies have largely abandoned the social markers that served to delineate and define transition from childhood into adulthood which, according to Malidoma Patrice Some (1994), are based on the principle that: 'A person who doesn't get initiated will remain an adolescent for the rest of their life'.

Some socialisation processes based on alternative cultures that exist can be described as old rites and others as new rites based on Western notions of development. (Goggins-II, 1998) (Blumenkarntz and Gravazzi, 1993; Myers, 1988). Schools provide the nearest equivalent western model of a traditional life cycle socialisation process (Richards, 2007). This formal and institutionalised education is currently fixed on attaining government-imposed key stage exam results. This is scarcely conducive to taking account of the spiritual, the ancestral or the interconnectedness which operate in African, Asian and other cultures.

There is an African proverb: 'It takes a whole village to raise a child'. If the school is the village and the teachers the elders, similarities can be built to match a traditional rites model that Hill (1992) describes as the 'new rites'. In the school environment teachers and mentors can work together in roles which are similar to advocates' or big brothers' or sisters' roles. This is not to suggest that teachers become family but that in many models of good practice they operate in an encouraging, nurturing and supportive role for their pupils.

Hill (1992) outlines the characteristics of old rites and new systems:

The Old Rites	The New Rites
Religious	Usually secular
Ran by sun and seasonal time (outdoor and active)	Operate by clock and calendar (usually sedentary and pursued behind closed doors)
Centred on concrete experiences	Rely heavily on words and abstractions
Provided physical risks and danger	Substitute organised sports, which combine moderate challenge and minimal risk
Dramatic, intense, forceful and fast	Slow, drawn out and often value only the ultimate destination
Engendered awe	Commonly produce detachment and boredom
Resulted in immediate and unmistakable status change	Provide no such direct deliverance into adult roles and status
Ended at a determined place and at a determined time, witnessed by the community as a whole	Can go on indefinitely, leads to dropping out, being pushed out (exclusion) perhaps never resulting in general community recognition (graduation with qualifications)

Figure 8.1 Old and New Rites of Passage

Mainstream school-based professionals appear to favour inflexibility – a response to restrictive government guidelines – and seldom perceive or interpret the multi-dimensional aspects and experiences of adolescents who live in the multiple contexts of the school, wider society, youth culture and home.

Rites of passage offer an alternative process of maturation through ages and stages. Rites take place over varying lengths of time, during which elders and initiates share some intensive experiences. Often they start long-lasting relationships. There is mutual respect of roles within the relationships with self, family and community. Value systems and areas of responsibility are shared. This centrism-based approach (see chapter 1), which locates the person as subject, as in alternative rites of passage programmes, is an orderly method of supporting transitional relationships within self, families and communities.

Multicultural paradigms include recognising non-linear causality instead of the European logic in which this is always followed by that – an alternative concept that everything affects everything. An alternative approach recognises the interrelatedness and interdependency of people and systems. It also makes the value of social and cultural contexts explicit. It values interpersonal relationships and subjectivity as well as objectivity.

In traditional rites of passage programmes the leaders are the elders. Like inclusive practitioners, elders are from different disciplines. The work can be demanding and the rewards huge in terms of making a positive difference to the lives of the young people.

Techniques of guidance and counselling are also closely connected to questions of value. The western concept of value as defined by the founders of humanistic, cognitive behavioural and psychodynamic psychologists informs the guidance and counselling for social inclusion. But these therapies overstress the 'I'-ness and the techniques concentrate on the here-and-now, whereas the elders subscribe to belief systems that prefer a close relationship between 'I' and 'we' and use metaphysical, intuitive, meditational approaches when working with young people.

Majors (2001) argues that emotional literacy is another quality which professionals need to operate in a socially inclusive way. Trained professionals need certain personal characteristics such as resilience if they are to ensure engagement and communication. Bergin's systematic analysis of theistic/religious and clinical-humanistic models reports that 'counsellors trained in institutions which embody clinical/ humanistic values may lose touch with their clients' (1980). This supports the importance of emotional literacy.

The frame of reference model brings together people and systems with a common theme of development. Without people, systems cannot work and without the systems people cannot be fully effective. The rites of passage developmental model presented here is a transferable framework for inclusive practice. The model reverses the existing approach used by schools – which is punitive, blames the child and places the burden of change and justice in the hands of the adults with the greatest influence in the life of the pupil.

Examples of socially inclusive practice

Teachers who work in mainstreams school were asked what strategies they have for raising the achievement of their Caribbean African students. This is what they said:

I found that rather than shout, if I talk and ask why, I meet less resistance.

I try to use sense of humour, if appropriate, to break the ice, it makes it easier.

I try to be less authoritarian as a first stance, without being too casual.

I try to put my own emotions aside.

I know my colleagues say it might be a gender issue but I think that is wrong, they are children and I am an adult. Gender is an excuse.

I provide positive role models to show them that they can achieve something great.

I give examples of how we got through when we were studying e.g. late nights, less socialising.

I do not see their exuberance as a problem; it is just their excitement.

Things always used to end up confrontational, until I saw myself as the common denominator and worked out that I was refusing to be flexible and they were saving face.

I set clear boundaries for expectations and I am fair and consistent with every one.

We have created a web-based hall of fame with photos and excerpts to show achievement in our schools. We work hard to make sure the images are representative of the entire school population.

These quotes are taken from interviews with teachers who are striving to be more inclusive. Others recognised the value of inclusive practitioners:

They [inclusive practitioners] talk to all different kinds of people and they link in with all different types of people ... that's the brilliant thing about it ... if you need help, they're never too busy to help you. If they can't help they point me in the right direction ... that's the crucial thing about it. (Police Officer, Youth Offending Team)

They [inclusive practitioners] work very well in conjunction with the teachers in the school. All the Heads value the services very highly indeed. (Headteacher)

The key findings of my research

School can cause anxiety in parents, pupils and practitioners. The Caribbean African population in particular are struck by how resistant schools can be to exploring the possibility that not all pupils receive equal treatment. Despite considerable research, some schools feel stigmatised by any suggestion that they excessively exclude African boys.

Parents are traumatised by their children's exclusion from school and struggle to remain dignified in the face of what for them is obvious social injustice. This trauma can render many of them non-functioning and they may well become depressed when they realise they cannot protect their children.

I found that because of their own negative school experiences, some parents are less able than previous generations to prevent the exclusion of their children. This may be a direct result of unresolved issues with schooling, or because the strength that is passed on in systems of cultural transference is missing or damaged. Some communities have inherited the legacy and consequences of a denied education. Children are being excluded both formally or informally, separated from normal classroom teaching, and their parents cannot defend them because the systems of appeal are unclear, they lack confidence or their concerns are dismissed. When parents become distressed about the treatment of their children at school they are accused of being emotional and find themselves defending their own reactions as well as their child. This happens disturbingly frequently and was voiced by many of those I spoke to. Parents are often fearful that if they challenge the school their child will be penalised.

There was a strong feeling from parents that if they can be imprisoned for keeping children off school, teachers should be subject to the same penalties for withholding education from children without justification.

My research concludes that exclusion as a punishment is not applied equally to all pupils who do not conform. The severity of the punishment is affected by the race and gender of the child. So discrimination appears to be based on something other than behaviour because not all children receive the same severity of punishment for the same behaviour.

General recommendations

There is a good deal that can be done to make schooling socially inclusive and educationally relevant to healthy adulthood and income generation. The FORMULA set out in Chapter 7 and illustrated on page 104 offers a framework to aid a systematic approach to inclusion. It is grounded in the findings of this research.

These further general recommendations are followed by recommendations to specific groups.

- The first step in preventing exclusions could be to appoint a government adviser with a specific portfolio for tackling the complex issues revealed by my research. This one act would send a message of commitment to a population who has been betrayed and disproportionately affected by school exclusion.

- Ofsted and the Department for Children, Schools and Families (DCSF) should work closely with diasporan African community organisations that are already working at grass roots level.

- High achievement among disadvantaged groups needs to be normalised. Confidence building should be part of an ongoing programme to recruit and empower parents to do their part to reclaim our young people. The programme would strive to help parents to find their voice and establish appropriate ways to communicate their concerns to schools and other education service providers.

- Appropriate and culturally sensitive rites of passage programmes should be available to all schools and every vulnerable child. Only culturally competent role models who reflect the population most disadvantaged should deliver such rites of passage programmes. They would include safety mechanisms to ensure that every child attained a high level of holistic human existence.

■ Pride in African children's cultural, spiritual, historical, intellectual and geographical heritage should be instilled in an effort to help them value themselves. School trips to places of relevance to the school population should be considered instead of the customary trips to Europe. A balanced world history should be compulsory in the curriculum.

■ The relationship between religion and spirituality should be explored.

■ A strategy to cultivate independent enquiring minds, creativity and entrepreneurship should be formulated and implemented.

■ Emotional literacy should be cultivated in parents, practitioners and pupils. Young people should be encouraged to find beauty and value in their heritage, community and self. They should be guided to become entrepreneurial, exploiting for the good of mankind the innate gifts they were born with. They should be helped to understand, interpret and articulate their reality.

In addition

■ Principles of healing should guide the process of working with a marginalised community, the first rule being to recognise and address the injury in this way the wound can be cleansed and tended and a learning environment created that stimulates healing

■ Self-development and professional development should be funded to ensure that all practitioners are aware of different approaches to working with people and can separate their own needs from the needs of their client group

■ Administrators should receive training to develop administrative skills that are flexible enough to meet the needs of the client group and the specialist practitioners operating in the field of social inclusion

■ Partnerships among professionals and with parents should be constructive, working, interrelated, multi-disciplined, flexible and mutually respectful

- Differentiation between services should be more rigorous. My research found some evidence of service overlap: the government funds several agencies that service the same geographical area and target groups, and these were in effect competing for limited funds. Restructuring into Children's Centres may ease this problem

- Relationships should be developed with the home, carer and community to allow early signals of exclusion risk to be detected. A shared language that facilitates non-threatening dialogue and better understanding would reduce errors which impact on the life chances of children

- Nationalised networks and local links should be formed to facilitate the sharing of good practice, innovation and effective interventions

- Socially inclusive practice should be supported by trainers to create specialist teams of seconded personnel who share practices, cross boundaries and can thus be more responsive to their client groups. Continuing professional and personal development should tackle the problems of professional envy

- Training programmes should be compulsory for mentors, parents, social workers, youth workers and other practitioners who work with young people. All must have access to network sources, policy development and practical ideas for engaging and including young people, sharing knowledge, resources and information and ensuring continuity

- The government allocates funds to schools based on certain formulae. The two most relevant to inclusion are the funds for vulnerable young people and ethnic minority achievement. Schools should use such funding for inclusion initiatives only.

Recommendations for recruiting teachers

We need to recruit the best possible applicants from the widest possible pool but, more importantly than teachers who are just African, we need teachers

- who are prepared to explore a model of education that is human centred and reflects the society and in particular the school pupil population

- with initiative who think for themselves and can interpret government guidelines to embrace inclusive practice

- who will use their knowledge, experience and compassion in imparting knowledge

- who are culturally sensitive African and Caribbean African adults who can add value to British schools

- who seek guidance and avoid protecting or massaging their own ego

- who realise the seriousness consequences of making a decision to exclude as opposed to considering the lifetime effect of their actions on a child's life chances

- who refuse to take part in execution style courts that present lists of children's misdemeanours to unsuspecting parents and vulnerable young people

- who do not allow their career aspirations to make them into people with hard heads, cold hearts, inhumanity and who do not absolve themselves of responsibility for the life chances of the young people entrusted to them

- who confront and eliminate all policies and acts of discrimination

Recommendations for policy makers

Policy makers should give schools and practitioners detailed information about joined-up thinking on socially inclusive principles and what it looks like in practice. In addition to the implications for inset training, school climate and organisational change, policy makers need to examine the current climate of target setting and consider how the model identified here can be reconciled with a culture which is competitive and thus excluding.

Inclusive policies direct practice away from the punitive approaches to discipline that culminate in exclusion. They promote a humanitarian approach to human interaction in schools and encourage ways in which to include and educate young people. Policy needs to be adapted that places these factors at the forefront.

Conclusion

Socially inclusive practitioners employ creative ways to engage pupils, possibly outside normal classroom time and to communicate with parents. They engage in professional development to keep themselves abreast of relevant issues. They are the special teachers you always remember because they see potential in their students – the teachers who, when you don't understand something, come back and explain it in a new way, with patience and sensitivity.

Inclusive teachers touch you and awaken your spirit, your creativity and open up myriad possibilities. They see their role as to bring out your potential. Traditional didactic pedagogy can isolate aspects of the person. It can isolate colleagues who are from different professional disciplines. This research indicates that socially inclusive practice is a beneficial and holistic approach to teaching which fosters personal and professional development, confidence building. It can entail meditation, movement, music, stress relievers, humour, honesty, humility, history, potential, high expectations and collaborative working but its most profound contribution is to consider the significance of every human being. Using the model of social inclusion makes the world of school a more humanitarian place.

Making a difference in the lives of young people is a human-to-human thing. Joy DeGruy Leary (2005) describes it as a person centred axiology that operates at micro level when teachers know the importance of the part they play in turning a child's life around and giving them the opportunity to go through the doors to their future life empowered.

In the final chapter I offer recommendations for parents whose children are at risk of exclusion or have been excluded from school.

9

The way we see it

The call for a difficult conversation between parents, policy makers, teachers, youth workers and other practitioners is made throughout this book. The conversation would tackle inequalities based on skin colour, class and gender. It would seek to deal with all the deep rooted issues that result in exclusion and take on board the perspectives of not only those that exclude but those that are excluded.

The conversation would explore the responsibility of adults to work in partnership to reduce exclusion whilst recognising its sensitive and complex nature, its causes and consequences. The challenge is how we proceed with this discourse. My research indicates that we need to evolve and embrace a pedagogy that facilitates acknowledgement, healing, knowing and growing of all those who believe in equal rights.

Certain conditions are essential. The first is an **African-centred pedagogy**, one that:

- legitimises alternative stores of knowledge
- positively exploits and scaffolds productive community and cultural practices
- extends and builds upon the indigenous language
- reinforces communities and encourages service to family, community and the world
- promotes positive social relationships

145

- imparts a worldview that idealises a positive self-directed future without denying the self-worth and right to the self-determination of others

- supports cultural continuity while promoting critical consciousness.

- promotes the knowledge of self and heritage

- recognises spirit as primary

- acknowledges world history

Although not defined explicitly in these terms, these pedagogies are intrinsic to the aims of social inclusion initiatives and have informed their practices.

Secondly, the issues of racial discrimination and exclusion from school needs to be kept in the public eye. Diane Abbott continues to keep them on the agenda with her annual conference, London Schools and the Black Child. But the conferences and the research come too late for the thousands of children who have been failed by their school and excluded, possibly on the whim of a teacher who has no idea of the effect of school exclusion on the life of Caribbean African students, or of a racist teacher who wealds power by abusing their authority and then becomes indignant when challenged.

Toyin Agbetu, founder and head of social policy and research at Ligali, a non-profit organisation, works with colleagues to keep the issue of educational inequality on the agenda in the media. Agbetu told online news media Black Britain, that how Africans are portrayed in the mainstream media is different to the way in which African people would present themselves.

> A black person constructed in the media has three attributes: they are involved in criminality, involved in sports or involved in entertainment. Anything that goes outside of those classifications is not of interest to the media. (January 31 www.blackbritain.co.uk (2007))

Many teachers do phenomenal work, especially in the pre-school and primary sectors, but just as in every other area of work there are some who take pleasure in inappropriately wielding their power over the lives of young vulnerable people.

The research statistics that were intended to highlight the phenomenon of excessive exclusion are now used as evidence to pathologise children and permit teachers to exclude them under the cloak of professional respectability afforded by schools. But for fairness to become embedded in educational practice, there has to be a radical paradigm shift away from a blame culture. Blaming will do little to address exclusion.

Government authorities know what is happening because of the extensive research that reveals the extent to which exclusion is affecting certain communities, especially African boys. Somehow the concern does not appear great enough to declare a national emergency.

The issues of school exclusion, anti-social behaviour, lost opportunities, unemployment, injustice, teenage pregnancy, crime, ill-health, poverty are closely linked. It is hoped that my research will be used to benefit my community by having an impact on how the government and other interested parties respond to all marginalised school populations. Using the FORMULA outlined in Chapter Seven and illustrated on page 104, this book concludes with recommendations of the practical steps that can be taken. These have emerged from the voices of a community marginalised, pathologised and vulnerable to school exclusion. This is their voice.

Recommendations for parents

You have a major role to play in giving your children the chance they deserve. Research statistics indicate that you could find yourself with an excluded child, especially if you have an African boy. Before matters reach this stage your child may experience other forms of injury. He may show signs of distress at home, such as adopting delaying tactics when it is time for school, becoming school phobic or avoiding eye contact. The school may have compiled a dossier of misdemeanours. Before or after exclusion you may undergo what will feel like an interrogation by a governing body or a special group with delegated powers to deal with exclusion. Such committees will often simply rubber stamp the will of the head teacher and possibly ruin the life chances of the child.

Make yourself familiar with and share the FORMULA on page 104. Photocopy it. You must be proactive: this means actively participating in all areas of your child's school experience. If you are passive, you will be subject to the wishes of others. Never relinquish your God-given role as parent or guardian. You know your child as no teacher can. Be persistent in requesting positive information about your child. If you become concerned put your concerns in writing and request a written reply. Hold the school accountable for your child's well-being and academic achievement. Counter the power of teachers with the rights of your child. Remember you are probably the only person for whom your child is top priority: teachers will tell you that they have other pupils to consider. Teach your child their history.

Your child will alert you to the fact that something is wrong. Or you may be bombarded with phone calls and letters of complaint from the school. Schools have hundreds of children on their register and so seldom ring parents – if you start receiving phone calls and letters, your child is at great risk.

If your child is excluded you have a right to appeal, so ask immediately for information about the procedure for appeal. Should you attend a meeting with the school you may have to face the excluding professional, a board of school representatives ranging from class teacher, SENCO (special needs coordinator), head of year, learning mentor, head teacher, school governor, inclusion personnel or anyone else the school feels they should invite. They may not warn you of who will be present. Do not be deterred or intimidated, take an advocate or 'friend' with you; remember you are fighting for the school career and life chances of your child.

This experience can be oppressive and overwhelming so be sure to take an informed and culturally sensitive parent advocate with you. This can be a friend, a professional or anyone who can witness and where appropriate represent your position.

As parents we play the central role in giving our children the chance they deserve. Sometimes the going will get tough so seek out advocates and associates who can support you.

Prevention is better than cure
Here are nine strategies to minimise the risk of your child being excluded from school

■ Talk with your child and his teacher to ensure that your perception of him is correct. Teachers teach in different ways but

148

should always be respected and respectful. Sometimes our perception of teachers and our children needs checking out. Perhaps you can agree a plan of support for your child together. The paradigms operating are not necessarily African-centred and this can place the African experience on the periphery of understanding. Nuclear families are a recent European social construct whereas Africans have traditionally lived in family units in village contexts. Draw on your community resources such as a supportive place of worship, social events, workshops, conferences and publications which reflect similarities to you and your child. Many schools are happy to have positive relationships with community-based organisations. It is your responsibility to ensure that you help the school develop a relationship with these organisations. Develop a four-pronged approach to parenting a school-aged child:

☐ be prepared to challenge anything you consider is not in the interest of your child

☐ trust your intuition and have faith in your child's potential

☐ keep your emotions in check

☐ show up at the school by appointment, but also unexpectedly and regularly. Attend every parents' evening, governing body meeting, school fete, summer fayre or community invitation or, if you can't, have someone represent you and the interests of your child

▓ Take everything to do with your child's education seriously: do not believe exclusion or injustice can never happen to you or your child. Learn to listen diligently to your child. Notice the music he listens to. Listen to the lyrics they spit (chat) on the mic. Take note of street identities or email tags

▓ Build positive relationships with your child's teachers and other members of the school community to ascertain their vision for your child. Discover your child's aspirations and use them to motivate him. Build relationships with him and the school-teachers so that communication is constant whether things are going well or not. Be consistent in your school communication. Spend time with your child where you are purposely talking less and listening more. Discover what his concerns are. Insist that the school communicate any matters of concern in writing, and you do the same

■ Tap into the aspirations of your child to motivate him and also to get an idea of how you can match the vision of yourself and him with the objectives of the school

■ Let the school know that you are aware of the exclusion risks for your child and that it is their responsibility to make sure he is not victimised or marginalised. Request access to all school records. Create a calendar of school meetings so that everyone involved is held accountable for his education

■ Become part of existing networks like the parent teacher association (PTA) and the school governing body. Join any local community groups that can enhance a positive school experience for your child

■ Ensure that you and everyone else have high expectations of your child, academically as well as socially

■ Empower yourself by attending events like conferences and support groups for parents so you can intervene and support your child continually and not just at times of crisis.

■ Attend culturally sensitive parenting classes that deal with the issues that affect your community and be prepared to learn from others if necessary.

Recommendations for practitioners

You are the face of the school or EOTAS – education otherwise than at school. You determine the educational experience for children and families whether you are based in a school or a community-based initiative. The children's future rests in partnership with you. Teaching and governance of the school is not simply about rubber-stamping: it is about accountability to parents and families and they rely on fair treatment. Do some self-searching: do you hold any opinions that might bias your perception or practice? Adopt practical strategies for reducing excluding practice:

■ Discover the local world of your students. Some practitioners parachute into schools and out again, so can't draw on local knowledge to underpin effective learning experiences for the pupils. Celebrate African history month, festivals and events and the significant cultural events on the calendar through the year. Engage in authentic participation.

▨ Be resilient in your efforts to communicate. Remember that the staffroom can sentence a pupil by labelling them. Avoid making unguarded negative comments which can subliminally influence colleagues.

▨ Share your vision for the pupils' success with them, their parents and colleagues.

▨ Put in place systems such as meetings, baseline assessments, pupil support plans and allocated key workers to ensure checks and balances according to agreed targets for pupils and parents, and include yourself in this monitoring programme. Don't be a martyr and try to do everything on your own. Work in partnership with other agencies where appropriate. Introduce performance indicators.

▨ Maintain your continuing professional development (CPD), develop your skills and knowledge and hold high expectations of yourself and your pupils. Tap into alternative, non-threatening and creative ways of getting information to and from students, parents and colleagues. Become culturally competent.

Recommendations for policy makers

Your policies inform the practice and provide the loopholes that excluding teaching practice can comfortably slip through. The importance of policy holders in reducing exclusion cannot be over-emphasised. Look at your influence and decide whether your policies

▨ are informed by research or by stereotypically biased influences

▨ are relevant and sensitive to the world of those affected by the policy

▨ are couched in the language of and responsive to the worlds of pupils, parents and professionals

Ask yourself:

- Do policies inter-relate? Are they joined up or disjointed?

- How can the existing policy frameworks accommodate new policies?

- Do policies feed into the earlier versions in a progressive way?

- Do policies promote excellence and high expectations of teachers as well as of children and their families?

- Do policies allow for flexibility and for culturally sensitive applications?

Recommendations for politicians

The lead set by parents, Diane Abbott and Ken Livingstone is to be applauded. They repeatedly and publicly commit to keeping school exclusion on the agenda. How are you supporting the needs of marginalised young people in education? These are the things politicians can do:

- Identify whether combating school exclusion is on your party agenda

- Support other politicians who are working to bring equality to all students

- Decide whether to toe the party line or make a difference in the community you serve

- Get in touch with the needs of your constituents and promote the rights of children

- Visit the schools in your area and speak to staff, pupils and parents or guardians outside your canvassing calendar. View schools as communities of people and listen to what they say

- Make efforts to create two way communication channels

- Include education as a human right in your political manifesto and feature detailed steps toward educational inclusion in your campaigns

- Put in place systems for monitoring the real life experience of school children – the future voters. The society of tomorrow depends on their school experience today

- Work with statutory and non-statutory, public and private sector individuals and community organisations to establish working links for change

- Develop your political argument in line with the honest feedback you get from children and parents as well as teachers and local and central government

- Be accessible and accountable to all your constituents and demonstrate genuine concern for the children and parents who do not have a voice but have been subject to social injustice by the school. Be their voice at the highest political level.

The research community

Researchers inform policy and politics. It is incumbent upon researchers to stop pathologising young people and perpetuating the idea that they are the problem. More attention needs to be focused on the profile of the teacher who reaches for exclusion as the first point of control or discipline. It is the fear of exclusion which prevents parents and pupils from pointing out the practitioners who cannot work with young people or don't even like them. Researchers need to be brave and push the boundaries of knowledge to examine this phenomenon from new perspectives and provide fair research that speaks to all involved in the process. We should ask ourselves these questions:

- Is our research data recent, relevant and rooted in relevant paradigms?

- Are we informed by qualitative and quantitative data or is our research statistic-led in a way that ignores the experience of those affected by exclusion?

- Can research institutions work harder to disseminate solution-focused research on matters of discrimination?

- Are we part of a research community that promotes and stimulates debate around discrimination or might we have lost touch and be basking in academic acknowledgement and reputation gained years ago?

- Are we monitoring and evaluating our own research approach?

■ Are we linked into local, national and international research? Are we being informed by and informing the existing knowledge about school exclusion?

■ Are we staying abreast of new knowledge that includes alternative subjugated knowledge systems?

■ Can our research offer solutions or are we focusing only on the problem?

Conclusion

Until images of African people appeared in American publications like *Ebony, Jet* and *Essence* magazine, recently beauty was always portrayed as white, slim, blonde and blue-eyed. There was never any information to tell me about the great achievements of African people. Once I discovered that most publications were avoiding using African images or distorting those they used so that African people seemed ugly, my interest in the experiences of African people became paramount.

Even as a child, when I heard the story of the ugly duckling, it struck a chord with me. I loved the message: that the ugly duckling suffered jibes, exclusion and humiliation because it was not recognised for what it was. It was one of the earliest times I realised how much I detest injustice and inhumanity. The ugly duckling was actually a cygnet – a beautiful elegant baby swan that had been mistaken and misunderstood, described according to the aesthetic and social norms of ducklings. The essence of the message is that the measure of beauty is relative to one's own community.

I see a similar scenario whenever African children are misunderstood and excluded, their beauty and worth judged relative to Europeans. On reflection, I realise that I did notice the disproportionate application of discipline when I was at school; I noticed that the school experience for young African males was often unfair and even excessively hostile.

Despite well intentioned warnings from colleagues that to once again raise the largely unspoken issue of racism in education is professional suicide, I am feeling the fear and doing it anyway, to present the undiluted perspective of a marginalised community. This has forced me to overcome my own issues of inadequacy about constructing English well enough to present it to an international publisher with sufficient foresight and commitment to provide a space for the voiceless. I have resisted advice to sanitise my findings. Instead I have presented the views of a marginalised and voiceless community that I come from and belong to and so have been privileged enough to observe as an insider and represent from an African-centered vantage point.

For over 30 years I have collected data in Europe, Asia, Africa and America and have now presented the findings in this book. They show that schooling is having a negative effect on thousands of families and this is hampering their ability to access resources and create strong sustainable communities.

I found that children enter playgroup largely innocent, trusting, eager, fresh-faced, exuberant and excited, even if a tad anxious about leaving their primary carer. They begin by encountering difference, sharing, colour, play, textures, rhyme and social interaction. However, as they move through nursery, reception, year 1 and so on, their school experience changes. The focus is on the curriculum, on literacy and numeracy targets. There is less interest in the human experience. By the time they reach high school the environment is markedly different, with the shouting of orders and in some cases a punitive ethos where children are expected to accept the power relationship between teachers and pupils unquestioningly. As they get older they are plunged into a loose college structure. They can become lost in the wilderness if they have no compassionate tutorial support and are not helped to develop the study skills and exam techniques essential for academic and vocational success. Consequently they enter the world and the workplace at a disadvantage.

People need to protest every time they encounter injustice, arrogance, bigotry or ignorance. Line managers who try to penalise those who are seeking to improve matters for pupils should be exposed and made accountable for their actions. They must realise that power is best shared and that it should lie with parents, pupils and practitioners as well as themselves.

There is an apalling silence about the reasons for the high exclusion rate. Practitioners claim that the causes are not entirely clear. I have taken part in conferences and radio debates where teachers insist that they feel under attack when parents describe instances of being harshly treated by schools. Teachers hijack empathy and marginalise the voice of the excluded. Their indifference, defensiveness and attempts to re-direct sympathies away from the children they harm looks to the Carib-bean African community like a calculated dismissal of the concerns of Africans, as having less importance than those of the dominant culture.

The school experience of thousands of Caribbean African children in the UK today is not what it should be. At a recent conference I listened whilst African professionals expressed the concerns they share with African parents. All have serious anxieties about the experience their children and grandchildren will have in British schools. A lead profes-sional working in the field of raising Caribbean African achievement confessed that her anxiety levels rose when she heard that her African grandchild was a boy! Other professionals were embarrassed to admit that there is a certain relief when a new African baby is a girl.

> We are the primary educators and I don't even think we should send our children to school. We should home school. We know we are treated un-fairly. Black men are considered a threat – and take mental health, we are more likely to be restrained. Attacking the male is a well known strategy in psychological warfare and racist systems. (Caribbean African parent)

The truth is that discrimination is systemic in the school system. The issue is not just about language, culture, class and colour: it is about systems of oppression. The consequence is unrest, resentment, illiteracy, unemployment and unearned privilege for the few.

The privileged who permit the discrimination against people to con-tinue may not easily come to the rescue of the voiceless, because that requires them to relinquish their position. The responsibility rests with those of us who believe in equality.

The impact of my study on myself

What my research has revealed has caused me much pain. It is painful to write and painful to read. Although I collected and analysed the data myself, I was still shocked by the evidence of what goes on daily in UK schools.

Many people shut down when they discover painful information and no doubt the teaching profession will resist the findings of my research. This will not help the plight of a community who are consistently marginalised and although my heart sank on many occasions, I did not – and will not – shut down. In fact I was spurred on and became even more curious. The grim reality was a source of motivation for a thorny piece of research.

During the more difficult periods I would meditate and listen to music. From an African-centred place, the parallels between jazz, blues, rap, gospel, soul, mento, reggae and roots music became increasingly evident and another source of strength. These musical genres carried the voices of great African philosophers, prophets, the oppressed and marginalised. They were a mechanism to not only raise awareness but to act as a healing balm for the wounds of the dispossessed living in a hostile climate. Those wounds remain. Yet they are still largely unrecognised by those with unearned privilege (DeGruy Leary, 2005) and even some members of the disadvantaged communities suffering from the enduring legacy of forced geographical and cultural dislocation.

This research led me to speak with people from different countries and cities including Birmingham, Bristol, Leeds, Liverpool, Manchester, Nottingham, Reading and rural communities in Derby and Somerset. I discovered that many of us cannot go further back than our grandparents in our attempts to trace our heritage because inadequate records were kept. I also discovered that we have enough information to recognise that we share a common history. One where we were racially socialised. Many of us were streamed and schooled according to our cultural background, class, ethnicity and gender instead of according to our ability and potential. This feels like a violent assault.

Oral histories often die with the passing of elders. Grandparents do not want to tell us things that may further reveal the extent and nature of the exclusion they faced. This may be because they believe we can lessen the hurt by erasing the memory. This book releases the voices of those who have been hurt and continue to be hurt by the memory of their schooling, in the hope that it will contribute to change.

As a researcher, I am influenced by artiste Marvin Gaye, who asked 'What's going on?' It is a question all interested parties should ask themselves and their colleagues.

This work has been a life-changing project. Being a portal for unheard voices is my humble contribution to repaying, in part, my huge indebtedness to all those who have fought for human rights and justice for all.

My many years of diligent research have accumulated considerable data. The weight of evidence is overwhelming. A very unpleasant truth is exposed which is that punitive schooling plunges thousands of disadvantaged and vulnerable children into an education experience that can haunt them into adulthood.

The voices of the excluded are usually confined to the culturally sensitive and creative oral traditions of music, songs, rap and dub poetry. Those voices have merged the philosophies and worldview experiences of a marginalised people. It is my hope that this work will sit well with those custodians and keep their pleas for social justice alive. Especially following the incredibly insensitive and ill informed marking in 2007 of legislation that did not emancipate or benefit any African but instead glorified William Wilberforce. This served to further marginalise the memory of African Ancestors who lost their lives resisting enslavement and insulted the descendants of Africans who were colonised and made to work on plantations.

The ultimate personal impact of this book will no doubt reveal itself in due course, as educationalists read it and either shoot the messenger or hear the message.

Acknowledgements

I express my appreciation to all those who have helped me finish this work, in particular my family and those of you who informed this project. This is your testimony.

Also thank you to editor Cllr. Lorna Campbell and Gillian Klein for believing in this project and challenging me to produce a high quality piece of work. Thanks also to the rest of the team at Trentham Books.

Words cannot sufficiently convey the extent of gratitude I owe to my husband Baldy Adalton, for his patience and encouragement to begin, continue and complete this mammoth task. You continued to provide as I set about this labour of love for the voiceless. I acknowledge your sacrifices.

I am especially grateful to my precious children Kirk Sinclair and Iscelyn Monique who loved me enough to ensure I had a constant supply of hugs, kisses and feedback despite my long periods of absence. You are my gifts from God, sent to keep me balanced.

Everlasting thanks go to my first teacher, my phenomenal mother Mildred Lestine Headley who birthed and continues to guide and nurture me. Gratitude also goes to my earth father, Gladstone MacDonald Headley, a great African from Barbados and my first philosopher who made his transition in August 2002. Your teachings and high expectations continue to provoke and inform me. Thank you forever.

I Give Thanks to a powerful guardian and sister, Ngozi Headley-Fulani MA, who continued to support this work despite having a house fire, to my brothers David and Carlton, especially my older brother Ngoma 24 Carrot Silver Bishop who unknowingly alerted me to the need for this research. To my sister Maxine Claye for her gentle mother energy and my youngest sister Anthea Hart who kept me connected.

Thank you to all the Elders in the Diasporan community whom I hold in high esteem, including my community parents; Mother Mollie Hunte for her compassionate wisdom, Elder Willis Wilkie for his resilient wisdom also his departed wife Elder Edna Wilkie. I Give thanks also to Mother Jessica Huntley and Elder Eric Huntley for their reflective wisdom and for permission to access their Bogle L'Ouveture library.

Thank you also to Clive Thompson who stepped forward without questions and simply supported me when I was wilting.

I also owe a tremendous debt of gratitude to contributors past and present who were generous with their time and good wishes, without whose support it would not have been possible for this book to see the light of day. It is not possible to name everyone; nonetheless, I am grateful to every single person from and in Africa, the Caribbean, America, Europe and Asia who has helped me in word, thought, deed and prayer.

I express sincere appreciation to my supervisors Professor Roy Evans and Dr Kyoko Murakami.

Special thanks
To Elder Rudolph Smith, Elder Emily Gunter, Brian DeLord, Maria Dowd and the various youth development teams who allowed me access to parents, students and practitioners.

Thank you also to Dr Mekeda Graham, my mentor, sisterfriend and role model. I also extend appreciation to Dr Richard Majors for his support and intellectual debate.

This work would not have been completed in the time frame without the support of critical friends and fellow research students Dr Cathy Tissot, Dr Helen Holgate, Hilary Dodman, Dr Liz Collins, Dr Litsa Papadimitriou and Dr Anthi Vakali who shared their experiences honestly and openly. Also Berenice Miles and Theresa Knox for their suggestions. Shquestra Sitawi and Emerson Braithwaite I acknowledge the confidence you had in me long before I had it in myself. Thank you also to Professor Ray Paul whose seminars provided research insights. Thank you also to Tygur Defunks-Perry who encouraged me to become technologically independent. Thank you to Dr Perry Stanislas who shared his precious thesis so that I would know what uncompromising research looked like. Thanks also to colleagues Alistair George, Cynthia Jones, Royston John, Kwabena Brenya, Lloyd Bedeau, Jason Sassoa and Lanie I. Also I thank Merville Williams and Wesley Griffiths in Barbados for your help on the final furlong and Glenna George for your valuable feedback.

Thank you to the holistic scholars like Asthemari Batekun (School High Master), Abraham Gibson (Author and Poet), El Crisis for his hypnotic spoken word power and philosophical chanting of ancient mystical wisdom you were sent by the Ancients as a modern day diasporan west african griot also my community son Victor Okpeyukun (Animator and Time Traveller), members of The Colloquium Of African-Descended Academics and Practitioners also to Dr. William Lezlee Lyrics Henry and all of the exceptional scholars who were on standby and all the scholars who went before, paved the way and on whose shoulders I stand.

And to my Ancestors and Spiritual Guides and most importantly The Most High God, The first and last in all things, for my life and the blessing and privilege of this task. Selah, Ashe and Amen.

References

Adams, R (2002) *Social Policy for Social Work*. Hampshire: Palgrave

Akbar, D N (1998) *The Community of Self*. Florida: Mind Productions and Associates

Akbar, N (2002) *Natural Psychology and Human Transformation.* Florida: Mind Productions and Associates

Ani, M (1994) *Yurugu: an African-centred critique of European thought and behaviour.* Trenton NJ: Africa World Press

Asante, M K (1988) *Afrocentricity: the theory of science.* Trenton NJ: Africa World Press

Ashby, D M (2003) *From Egypt to Greece.* Florida: Muata Ashby

Bagihole B (1997) cited in Tregaskis C. *Constructions of Disability*. London: Routledge

Barrow, A G J (1986) *The Unequal Struggle*. London: Centre for Caribbean Studies

Bergin A (1980) Psychotherapy and Religious Values. *Journal of Consulting and Clinical psychology* 48(1)

Blair, M (2001) *Why Pick on Me: school exclusion and Black youth*. Stoke on Trent: Trentham Books

Bhavnani, R (2001) *Rethinking Interventions in Racism*. Stoke on Trent: Trentham Books

Blumenkrantz, D G and Gavazzi, S M (1993) Facilitating clinical work with adolescents and their families through the rites of passage experience program. *Journal of Family Psychotherapy* 4(2)

Bourne, J Bridges, L and Searle, C (1994) *Outcast England: How Schools Exclude Black Children*. London: Institute of Race Relations

Browder, A T (1989) *Browder File: 22 Essays on the African American Experience.* Washington: The Institute of Karmic Guidance

Browder, A T (1997) *Survival Strategies for Africans in America*. Washington: The Institute of Karmic Guidance

Bullock, S A (1975) *A Language For Life*. London: DfES

Campbell, H (1985) *Rasta and Resistance: from Marcus Garvey to Walter Rodney.* London: Hansib Publishing

Christian, M (2001) African Centered Knowledge: a British perspective. *The Western Journal of Black Studies* 25(1)

Coard, B (1971) *How the West Indian child is made educationally sub-normal in the British school system.* London: New Beacon Books

Comer, J P and Poussaint, A F (1992) *Raising Black Children.* New York: Penguin Books

Corrall, S (1992) *Self Managed Learning: the key to professional and personal development. Developing professionals in information work.* London: HMSO

Council of Europe (1995) *The European Convention on Human Rights.* Strasbourg: Council of Europe

Crotty, M (1998) *The Foundations of Social Science.* London: Routledge

CSIE, Centre for Studies on Inclusive Education (2000) *Index for Inclusion: developing learning and participation in schools.* London: CSIE Bristol and DfEE London

Daniels, H and Sellman, E (eds) (2003) *Study of Young People Permanently Excluded From School.* Birmingham: Department for Education and Skills

Dei, G J S (1999) *Spiritual Knowing and Transformative Learning.* Toronto: New Approaches to Lifelong Learning

Delanty, G (1999) *Social Theory in a Changing World: conceptions of modernity.* Cambridge: Polity Press

Dent, H C (1981) *Education in England and Wales.* East Sussex: Unibooks

Department of Education (1967) *Children and their primary schools.* London: HMSO

Department of Education and Science (1981) *West Indian Children In Our Schools.* Rampton Report. London: HMSO

Department of Education and Science (1985) *Education for All: report of the committee of enquiry into the education of children from ethnic minority groups.* Swann Report. London: HMSO

Department for Education and Employment (1994d) *Education Otherwise Than At School (EOTAS).* London: DfES

Department for Education and Employment (1999a) *Social Inclusion: pupil support circular 10/99.* London: DfES

Department for Education and Employment (1999b) *Circular 11/99.* London: DfES

Department for Education and Employment (1999) *National Curriculum Inclusion Statement.* London: DfEE.

Department for Education and Employment (2000) *National Statistics Bulletin.* London: DfEE

Department for Education and Employment (2001) *Statistics.* London: DfEE

Department for Education and Employment (2003) *Aiming High: raising the achievement of ethnic minority pupils.* London: DfEE

Department for Education and Skills (2003b) *Every Child Matters* (CM5860). London: DfES

Department for Education and Employment (2006) Priority Review: *Exclusion of Black Pupils: Getting it. Getting it right.* London: DfES

REFERENCES

Dhondy, F (1985) *The Black Explosion In British Schools*. London: Race Today Publications

Diop, C A (1978) *The Cultural Unit of Black Africa*. Chicago: Third World Press

Donaldson, M (1986) *Children's Minds*. London: Harper Collins

Fanon, F (1967) *Black Skin White Masks*. New York: Grove Press

Finkelstein V (1988) *Attitudes and Disabled People*. New York: World Rehabilitation Fund

Foucault, M (1975) *Discipline and Punish*. Brighton: Harvester Press

Foucault, M (1980) *Power/Knowledge*. Brighton: Harvester Press

Freire, P (1985). *The Politics of Education: culture power and liberation*. New York, Bergin and Garvey

Fuller, N (1971) *The United Independent Compensatory Code/System/Concept: a textbook/workbook for thought, speech and/or action for victims of racism (white supremacy)*. Neely Fuller Jr

Fulton, D and Upton G (1993) *Putting Problems In Context: taking issue*. London: The Open University and Routledge

Garvey, A J (1986) *The Philosophy and Opinions of Marcus Garvey*. Massachusetts: The Majority Press

Gillborn, D (1987) Natural Selection New Labour race and education policy. *Multicultural Teaching* 15(3)

Gillborn, D (1990) *Race, Ethnicity and Education*. London: Unwin Hyman

Gillborn, D (2001) Raising standards or rationing education? Racism and social justice in policy and practice. *Support for Learning* 16(3)

Gillborn, D and Gipps, C (1996) *Recent Research on the Achievements of Ethnic Minority Pupils*. London: Office for Standards in Education.

Gillborn, D and Mirza, H (2000) *Educational Inequality: Mapping Race, Class and Gender*. London: Ofsted

Gilroy, P (2002) *The Black Atlantic: modernity and double consciousness*. London: Verso

Gilroy, P (2006) *There Ain't No Black in the Union Jack*. Oxfordshire: Routledge

Gipps, H (1987) *Supporting Warnock's Eighteen Per Cent: six case studies*. East Sussex: The Falmer Press

Goggins-II, L (1998) *Bringing The Light Into A New Day*. Ohio: Saint Rest Publications

Gold, R D C (2002) *Running a School 2002/03*. Bristol: Jordan Publishing Limited

Gordon, G (2007) *Towards Bicultural Competence – beyond black and white*. Stoke on Trent: Trentham Books

Graham, M (2001) *Educating Our Black Children: new directions and radical approaches*. London: Routledge

Graham, M (2002) Creating Spaces: exploring the role of cultural knowledge as a source of empowerment in models of social welfare in Black communities. *British Journal of Social Work* 32(1)

Grace, G (1995) *School Leadership: beyond education management.* London: Rout-ledgeFalmer

Hall, S (Ed) (1992) *Formations of Modernity: understanding modern societies an intro-duction book.* Milton Keynes: Open University Press

Hans, N (1966) *New Trends in Education in the Eighteenth Century.* London: Cox and Wyman

Heidegger, M (1955) *What Is Philosophy?* London: Vision Press

Heimler, E (1982) *The Emotional Significance of Work. Concilium: unemployment and the right to work: 16-23*

Henry, W (2006) *What The Deejay Said: a critique from the street.* London: Nu-Beyond: Learning By Choice

Hill, P (1992) *Coming of Age: The African American Male Rites-of-Passage.* Chicago: African American Images

HMI (1985) *Better Schools.* London

Hodgdon, L (1999) *Solving Behavior Problems in Autism: improving communication with visual strategies.* Troy, Michigan: Quirk Roberts Publishing

Hollis, M (1997) *Invitation To Philosophy.* Oxford: Blackwell

Hyde, M (2000) *From Welfare to Work? Social Policy for Disabled People of Working Age.* London: Taylor and Francis

Hylton, C (1999) *African Caribbean Community Organisations: The Search for Indivi-dual and Group Identity.* Stoke on Trent: Trentham Books

Jeffers, S (1997) *Feel The Fear and Do It Anyway: how to turn your fear and indecision in to confidence and action.* Wales, Cygnus Books

Karenga, M (1990) *The Book Of Coming Forth.* University of Sankore

Leary, J D (2005) *Post-traumatic Slave Syndondrom: America's legacy of enduring injury and healing.* Oregan: Uptone Press

Levitas (1998) *Tackling Social Exclusion.* London: Routledge

Ligali (2007) http://www.ligali.org.uk

London Borough of Ealing (2004) *Collaboration and Change: working together to raise achievement of African-Caribbean children and young people.* London: LB Ealing

Macbeth, A (1993) Parent-Teacher Partnership – a minimum Programme and a Signed Understanding *Managing The Effective School* M Preedy. Buckingham: Open University: 193-203

Mackintosh, N J and Mascie-Taylor (1985) The IQ Question in *The Swann Report, Education for All.* London: HMSO

Macpherson, W (1999) *The Stephen Lawrence Inquiry: report of an inquiry by Sir William Macpherson of Cluny.* London: Stationery Office

Majors, R (2001) *Educating Our Black Children: new directions and radical ap-proaches.* London: Routledge

Mannheim, K (1936) *Ideology and Utopia.* New York: Harcourt, Brace and World

Maxwell, M (1968) Violence in the toilets. *Race Today* 1(5)

Mittler, P (2000) *Working Towards Inclusive Education*. London: David Fulton

Morris, K B E (1988) *Effective School Management*. London: Paul Chapman Publishing

Myers, L (1988) *Understanding an Afrocentric Worldview: Introduction to Optimal Psychology*. Dubuque: IA Kendall

Nantambu, K (1996) *Egypt and Afrocentric Geopolitics*. Ohio: Imhotep Publishing Company

Office for Standards in Education (1997) *Achieving Good Behaviour in Schools*. London: HMSO

Oliver, M. (1996) *Understanding disability: from theory to practice*. London: Macmillan.

Parsons C (2000) *Education, Exclusion and Citizenship*. London: Routledge Falmer

Patterson, S (1963) *Dark Strangers a study of West Indians in London*. London: Pelican

Peters, P (1975) *The Logic of Education*. London: Redwood Burn

Piggott, F M (1995) *Careers guidance and ethnic minorities in Holland and Britain – taking issue*. London: The Open University and Routledge

Pring, R (1978) Problems of Justification in Pring, R (ed) *Theory and Practice of Curriculum Studies*. London: Routledge and Kegan Paul

Qualifications and Curriculum Authority (2007) www.nc.uk.net/nc_resources/html/inclusion

Quansah, G in Blackman, M (2007) *Unheard Voices: the awakening of Elmina*. London: Random House

Ranson, S (1992) Towards a learning society. In *Education Management and Administration* 20(1)

Rassool, N and Morley L (2000) *School Effectiveness: fracturing the discourse*. London: Routledge

Reimer, E (1971) *School Is Dead*. London: Penguin Education

Richards, S (2002) How a person centred multi-sensory multidisciplinary approach to teaching and learning assists the achievement of 'disaffected' and/or 'at risk' students. Unpublished conference paper. Hertfordshire: University of Hertfordshire

Richards, S (2003) An emerging model of Social Inclusion Practice. Conference paper. Reading University

Richards, S (2003) Social policy and education inclusion. Conference paper. Nottingham University

Richards, S (2003) Practicing socially inclusion. CEDAR conference paper. Warwick University

Richards, S (2003) Inclusive practice: preliminary principles. Conference paper. London Metropolitan University

Richards, S (2004) Concept to Practice. Applied Inclusiveness: An Emergent Model of Socially Inclusive Practice. Thesis. Brunel University

Richards, S (2004) Examining practice. Conference paper. Brunel University

Richards, S (2004) Solution Focused Inclusion Delivery: empirical evidence. London Schools and The Black Child conference

Richards, S (2006) Re-orientation: the road to healing. Conference paper. London Metropolitan University: Separation and Reunion Forum (SRF)

Richards, S (2006) Who Cares? in *Nex Generation*. London: Nex Generation Media

Richards, S (2007) Difficult Conversations and Paradigm Shifting: a healing discourse. Conference paper. Southbank University

Richards, S (2007) The Enduring Metaphysical Legacy of an African Genocide. Conference paper. London Borough of Lambeth

Richards, S (2007) *The journey.* London: Reaching Out Development Services

Richards, S (2007) Replacing Western Psychologies of Education with Holistic Education. Conference paper. African Achievement Alliance

Richards, S (2007) *Post Traumatic Slave Syndrome in SPARK*. London: Hackney Council for Voluntary Service.

Richards, S and Headley-Fulani, N (2003) *Education Africa Teaching: The Report and evaluation.* London: EAT.

Richards, S and Wright, C (2004) *Pupil Exclusions* in London Schools and the Black Child III: Reaching for the Stars. Conference Report. London: Mayor of London

Richardson B (2005) *Tell It Like It Is: how our schools fail black children.* London: Bookmarks Publications and Trentham Books

Richardson, R and Wood, R (2000) *Inclusive Schools, Inclusive Society.* Stoke on Trent: Trentham Books

Ridgway (1972) *Recent Measures for the Promotion of Education in England.* Manchester: E J Morten publishers

Rossi, P H *et al* (2004) *Evaluation A Systematic Approach.* London: Sage Publications

Rustemier, S (2002) *Social and Educational Justice: The human rights framework for inclusion.* Bristol: Centre for Studies on Inclusive Education CSIE

Ryan, W (1976) *Blaming The Victim.* New York: Vintage Books

Scarman, Lord (1981) *The Brixton Disorders.* London: HMSO

Sewell, G (1986) *Coping with Special Needs.* London: Croom Helm

Sewell, T (1997) *Black Masculinities and Schooling: how Black boys survive modern schooling.* Stoke on Trent: Trentham Books

Shujaa, M J (1994) *Too Much Schooling, Too Little Education.* Trenton, New Jersey: Africa World Press

Simon, P (2006) *The Mystical and Magical Paths of Self and not-self.* London Tamare House Publishers

Slee, R and Allan, J (2001) *Excluding the Included: a reconsideration of inclusive education. International studies in sociology of education.* London: Routledge.

Social Exclusion Unit (1998b) *Truancy and School Exclusion.* Cm3957, SEU

Some, M P (1993) *Of Water and the Spirit.* Penguin Books.

Stokes, P (2003) *Philosophy 100 Essential Thinkers.* London: Arcturus Publishing

Stone, M (1981) *The Education of the Black Child in Britain: the myth of multiracial education.* London: Fontana

Stubbs, M (1976) *Language, Schools and Classrooms.* London: Methuen

UNESCO (1994) *The Salamanca Statement and Framework For Action On Special Needs Education.* Paris: UNESCO

van Sertima, I (1975) *They Came Before Columbus: The African presence in ancient America.* New York: Random House

Walker, R (2005) *When We Ruled.* London: Every Generation Media

Warnock, M (1978) *Report of the Committee of Enquiry into the Education of Handicapped Children and Young People.* London

Warnock, M (1988) *A Common Policy for Education.* Oxford: Oxford University Press

Welsing, F C (1995) *The Isis Papers.* Chicago: Third Word Press

Wenger, E (1999) *Communities of Practice Learning, Meaning and Identity.* Cambridge: Cambridge University Press

Wilson, A N (1992) *Awakening the Natural Genius of Black Children.* Afrikan World Infosystems

Wiredu K (1987). Wiredu on how not to compare African thought with western thought: A commentary. New Brunswick, *African Studies Review* 30(1)

Woodson, C G (1996) *Mis-education of the Negro.* New Jersey: Africa World Press

Wright, C (1992) *Race Relations in the Primary School.* London: David Fulton

Young, J Z (1978) *Programs of The Brain.* Oxford: Oxford University Press

Yuen, F K O (1999) Family Health and Cultural Diversity. *Family Health: A Holistic Approach to Social Work Practice.* Westport: Auburn House

Index